TO LOOK AT LIFE

AUTHOR	Bernardo Moya
TRANSLATOR	Jessica Epstein
EDITOR	Matthew Wingett
REVISION AND INDEXING	Paz Cabo
COVER DESIGN	Laura Thomson
LAYOUT	Duento
IMAGES	Shutterstock And Fotolia (Standard License)
ILLUSTRATIONS	Luis Serrano
PRODUCTION	Bernardo Moya

Published in 2014 by The Best You Ediciones, 3rd. Floor, 5 Percy Street, London, W1T 1DG

The partial or total reproduction of this book is strictly prohibited, as is its incorporation into any information system, and its transmission in any way or by any means, whether electronic, mechanical, by photocopy, recording, or other methods, without the prior written authorisation of the editor. Infringement of the aforementioned rights may constitute a crime against intellectual property (Article 270 et seq. of the Penal Code).

ACKNOWLEDGEMENTS

A word of thanks to all who have purchased this book and have given me the opportunity to enter your lives, to allow me to help you in some way.

I would like to thank my beloved wife, Julia, for all the support, trust, and love she has always bestowed upon me. She has been my mast, my sail, my rudder, and my compass. And I thank my children—Max, Lucci, and Gigi—who are my pride and legacy.

My most sincere gratitude to my friends for your support, and to my mother Antonia for being so strong, so brave, and amazing. I owe her and her unconditional love so much, in many ways …

In conclusion, thank you to all those who have supported and inspired me, and to the great thinkers who have given us such relevant and significant quotations.

Gratitude is the memory of the heart. **—Anonymous.**

INDEX

1. WHO SAID 'FEAR?' — 10
2. BE CONSCIOUS — 12
3. FORGET — 14
4. NEVER GIVE UP — 16
5. LEARN — 18
6. RELAX — 20
7. I LOVE YOU! — 22
8. INHALE–EXHALE — 24
9. HITTING ROCK BOTTOM — 26
10. WHAT DO YOU THINK? — 28
11. CURIOSITY — 30
12. OBSERVE — 32
13. BE MORE CHARISMATIC — 34
14. ENJOY LIFE — 36
15. SEATED OR STANDING? — 38
16. FRIENDSHIP — 40
17. VICES — 42
18. TODAY TOWARDS TOMORROW — 44
19. SILENCE — 46
20. CHANGE IT UP — 48
21. READ — 50
22. DON'T JUDGE — 52
23. GIVE A HUG — 54
24. TODAY — 56
25. LOSING WEIGHT — 58
26. TIME — 60
27. A WORTHWHILE DINNER — 62
28. MAINTAIN THE FLAME — 64
29. THE END OF THE WORLD — 66
30. SPRING IN YOUR STEP — 68
31. YOU ARE AN EXPERT — 70
32. IMPORTANT — 72
33. SMOKE, SMOKE … DIE, DIE… — 74
34. OBSERVE YOUR CHILDREN — 76
35. ACCEPT — 78
36. BE LIKE WATER — 80
37. INFERIOR — 82
38. FORGIVE — 84
39. WEEKEND — 86
40. EXCUSE ME — 88
41. RESULTS — 90
42. ARE YOU SILLY? — 92
43. COPY — 94
44. BE USEFUL — 96
45. VISUALISE — 98
46. LISTEN — 100
47. CONSPIRACY — 102
48. ACCEPT AND EMBRACE CRITICISM — 104
49. AN OPTIMISTIC BUT REAL FUTURE — 106
50. YOUNG OR OLD? — 108
51. BE GENEROUS — 110
52. WHAT'S YOUR OPINION? — 112
53. DO YOU BELIEVE? — 114
54. CAN YOU IMAGINE? — 116
55. BE RESOLUTE — 118
56. IMPATIENT? — 120
57. DO SOMETHING DIFFERENT — 122
58. HAPPINESS — 124
59. MEASURE YOUR WORDS — 126
60. WHAT TIME DO YOU HAVE? — 128

61. MAKE MISTAKES	**130**	93. MORE JOY	**196**
62. BE BLIND	**132**	94. LOST?	**198**
63. LIVE LIFE LIKE A MOVIE	**134**	95. BE DIFFERENT	**200**
64. ADVERSITY	**136**	96. YOU WILL DIE	**202**
65. YOUR JOURNEY	**138**	97. PLAN. SCHEDULE	**204**
66. PLANT A TREE	**140**	98. YOUR NEXT YEAR	**206**
67. WANT TO SUCCEED? WILL TO	**142**	99. LISTEN	**208**
68. TEACH–HELP–MENTOR–INSPIRE	**144**	100. IF YOU WERE SELLING YOUR LIFE …	**210**
69. MINOR FLAW?	**146**	101. MEET—COMMUNICATE	**212**
70. ENVY SOMEBODY?	**148**	102. FIND A COACH	**214**
71. ARE YOU MEDIOCRE?	**150**	103. YOUR WEALTH	**216**
72. DEVELOPED?	**152**	104. INNER SMILE	**218**
73. DOUBT	**154**	105. PRACTICE	**220**
74. WHAT AFFECTS YOU?	**156**	106. RESCUE YOURSELF	**222**
75. PICTURES ON YOUR WALL	**158**	107. LIMITING BELIEFS	**224**
76. HABITS	**162**	108. EMPOWERING BELIEFS	**228**
77. KNOWING	**164**	109. EXAGGERATE	**230**
78. DESTINY	**166**	110. IT DEPENDS ON YOUR POINT OF VIEW	**232**
79. TAKE A WALK	**168**	111. MOTIVATION	**234**
80. WANT TO REACH OLD AGE?	**170**	112. ACT	**236**
81. TIME	**172**	113. MAKE PLANS	**238**
82. WHAT SHALL WE EAT?	**174**	114. CRISIS	**240**
83. LOVE YOURSELF	**176**	115. THINK ABOUT A LOVED ONE DAILY	**242**
84. THE EPHEMERAL LIFE	**178**	116. FATHERLY LOVE	**244**
85. FACIAL MUSCLES	**180**	117. THINK 'HARRY POTTER'	**246**
86. HAVE A LAUGH!	**182**	118. THE FOUR SEASONS	**248**
87. 1%–100%	**184**	119. WHAT WOULD YOU DO?	**250**
88. BEAUTY	**186**	120. DON'T LIE TO YOURSELF	**252**
89. MANAGE YOUR MIND	**188**	121. RESILIENCE	**254**
90. GRATEFUL OR UNGRATEFUL	**190**	122. BE A WINNER	**256**
91. PRIORITIES	**192**	123. THE OBJECTIVE	**258**
92. PROBLEMS	**194**		

PROLOGUE
123 WAYS TO LOOK AT LIFE

During pivotal times such as the ones we are living in, when everything seems to be sinking beneath our feet and we struggle to find answers; when we live in a world that seemed stable and lasting until a few decades ago, one in which hundreds of civilisations have matured and amassed a body of knowledge which we have inherited, yet we lose some of it daily; when we live on a beautiful planet with a sun, a moon and oceans which have always claimed our love and which today we are concerned about potentially losing; in a time such as this, so fragile, we must change our perspective, and books such as *123 Ways to Look at Life*, by Bernardo Moya, are simply essential.

There are books which, upon having read them, we feel we are finished, and other books that live on in our memory. Some of the things we read arrive during crucial times in our lives and leave their mark on us, whereas others we scarcely remember because they were never really important. This book is directed to those who want to go through life truly living it, and not feeling as if they barely made it through. Bernardo Moya is known as one of the top professionals in the field of personal development. He is profoundly committed to education and growth, offering parents, professors, educators, businesspeople, and other individuals the necessary resources to help bring out the best in others.

Bernardo Moya emphasises the need, in this day and age more than ever, to have a positive attitude and the absolute confidence that personal objectives, dreams, and projects can be fulfilled.

123 Ways to Look at Life offers us keys to reprogramming our false and limiting beliefs. It leads us towards our goals, and convincingly shows us that we are travelling on the right path. It helps us to regain our true priorities through motivation, trust, love, and focusing on the true meaning of life.

This brief book, packed full of advice and quotes which affirm the marvellous culture which each and every one of us is a part of, invites us to drink fully from the cup of life, to enjoy it, and to play an active role within a collective of ideas, projects, and dreams which can lead us, together, towards new ways of feeling, learning, and looking at life. In brief, it allows us to enter into ourselves, in a brave yet subtle exploration, to discover our own confidence, our motivation, to determine what our priorities are, and to see what in our life has turned into a burden that we need to let go of.

This book is made up of short chapters, each with advice and quotes, and is a sort of 'manual' in user-friendly terms, humorous and persuasive. It draws on great thoughts expressed in the classics and by other contemporary authors. It includes narratives on personal discovery such as *Never Give Up, Observe, Accept, Be Like Water, Be Useful, Visualise, Listen*; sections on creativity and the internal struggle, among which the following stand out: *Be More Charismatic, Enjoy Life, Results, Accept and Embrace Criticism*; passages on emotions, such as *Happiness, Beauty, Have a Laugh, Inner Smile*; and many others addressing our confidence, family, love, charisma, friendship, time, and enjoyment of life. Bernardo Moya teaches, helps, mentors, inspires and convinces us!

One of the notable qualities of the books written by Bernardo Moya and one of the priorities of his publishers is their exclusively digital format. This allows the readers more room to cultivate their emotions with the aid of images which seem to live within the author's words. This virtual proximity to one's own thoughts allows us as the reader to enter into ourselves and to visualise our feelings. The accompanying audio book, read in a pleasant voice, is part of this process.

Perhaps it is the time for transformation, for revolution, as has been suggested by Álex Rovira; the time when crisis is an opportunity; the time for reinventing ourselves, for being reborn from our ashes, like the phoenix; for reprogramming our lives and our objectives, for becoming better, for re-feeling emotions we thought were forgotten; for recovering our imagination, for being stronger, for embracing and creating new projects. Certainly it may be time to see the future as Bernardo Moya recommends—smiling at life and letting go, at last, of the superfluous and of the limitations that make us feel small ... letting them go like those helium balloons that would slip through our fingers when we were children. Now we have 123 positive perspectives on life.

Paz Cabo
Editor, *The Best You Ediciones*

123 WAYS TO LOOK AT LIFE
INTRODUCTION

---

123 is for those who are looking for ideas, inspiration, guidance, motivation, and spark in their lives.

123 aims to provoke a reaction, to make you a little uncomfortable.

Seneca said: *It is not because things are difficult that we do not dare, it is because we do not dare that they are difficult.*

123 Ways to Look at Life is for those who are seeking ideas expressed in a short and powerful way, because 'few words to the wise are sufficient'. My priority is to make you think. I want to pique your curiosity, to help you question yourself, to dig deep, to think about 'what would happen if ...'

Having read from great authors and having attended professional courses through which I have tried to improve as a person, my desire with this book is to embed ideas, quotes, and techniques in your mind which will help you enjoy life more and to value what you have.

Thanks to this book, I have been able to see and appreciate the fact that, even though I am along in years, I still have much to learn.

This book is meant to help place value on the most important things. In these times of uncertainty, of tension, of difficulties, we must be focused on the small but significant things that make us what we are.

Whatever problem we may be faced with, in the end it's these fundamental things that count.

I have always been partial to quotations and statements by the great thinkers, those that are deep and inspired. For me, sometimes a single phrase is enough; I feel that it focuses and motivates me.

This is my intention with these quotes. And why 123? Why not? The number is not what's important. The important thing is that you undertake to apply one every day, every week, or however often works best for you. Experiment and practice.

Life is made of ups and downs, good times and difficult moments. The important thing is how you face them. In life, we must be willing to grow, to love, to change, to learn, to accept; to see, to listen, to respect, to observe; to forget, to forgive, to be grateful, to enjoy; in two words: to live! My hope is that you will apply each of the quotes that I recommend, even when some are or seem uncomfortable.

You cannot grow and develop if you know the answers before you ask the questions. —Wayne W. Dyer

1. Who said 'fear?'

Fight your fears. The act of overcoming something that bothers you or holds you back increases your confidence, and makes you stronger. Death overcomes us only once, and if we're lucky we won't even feel it. Fear can overcome us every day.

The future has many names: for the weak, it means the unattainable, for the fearful, it means the unknown. For the courageous, it means opportunity. —Victor Hugo

2. Be conscious

In the dictionary we find the following definition of consciousness:

· Feeling, thinking, and acting with awareness of one's actions and their repercussions.

· What one does under these conditions.

· Having full use of one's senses and faculties.

We should always be conscious, but often we are not. —Conscious of our emotional state, which we sometimes barely perceive; conscious of the repercussions of our words, of life, of living, which we often forget to think on.

Gustavo Estrada Luque said: *If you are not conscious of yourself and your reality, you journey through the emptiness of absence.*

I say: *Be conscious of your consciousness.* —**Bernardo Moya**

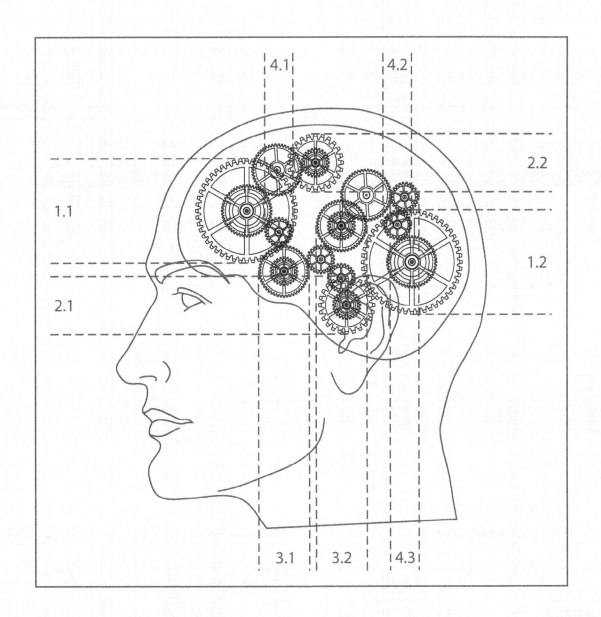

3. Forget

Seneca said: *Let us try to forget that which makes us sad when brought to mind.*

There are persons and situations which should be forgotten. When we create images or 'movies' in our mind reliving situations we have experienced, we can make them either more or less intense, based on how we choose to think about them. The simplest thing to do with them is to 'forget' them—to erase or to eliminate thoughts which affect us negatively. On your computer you have a 'delete' key. Think about the image or movie of that memory as being on your screen. You see it? Now press 'delete'. Done!

4. Never give up

Anthony Burgess, the novelist, was diagnosed with cancer at the age of 40. Wanting to leave a legacy for his family, he began to write. A year later, he had completed five novels. Surprisingly, his tumour went into remission and he lived more than 30 years after that. The world is full of similar stories. NEVER GIVE UP!

To give up is for the cowardly, but to surrender completely and face the consequences is for the brave. —**Anonymous**

5. Learn

What have you learnt today? What have you set out to learn today? What have you planned to assimilate this week? This month? This year? And in your lifetime? To grow as a person and an individual, it's necessary to educate yourself and study.

Make a list of things that you want to learn, and begin today!

An expert is a fellow who is afraid of learning something new, because then he wouldn't be an expert any more. —**Harry S. Truman**

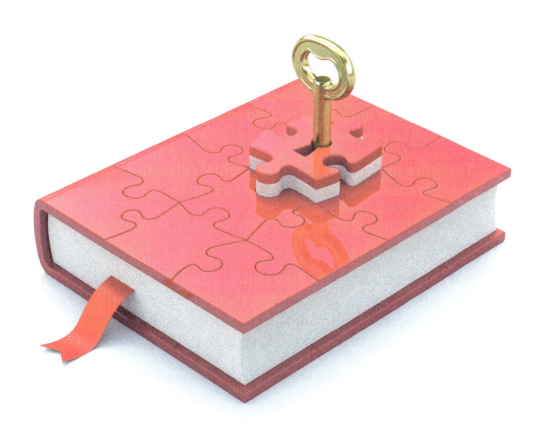

6. Relax

Sydney. J Harris said: *The time to relax is when you don't have time for it.*

Relaxing the body and the spirit is a wonderful thing that we should all experience. The daily practice of relaxation is considered very important for maintaining good health, both physical and mental. Mental relaxation normalises the body's equilibrium, reduces the production of hormones related to stress, and improves heart rate and arterial pressure.

There are many techniques for mental relaxation, such as yoga, tai chi, therapeutic massage, and visualisation.

Proper breathing is the first step towards reaching a state of complete relaxation.

It is important to know how to prioritise. We are so wrapped up in our daily tasks, in our routines, that we often do not place enough importance on taking time for ourselves and relaxing. Give yourself 15 minutes every day to relax, visualise, and think. Start today!

Hartman Jule said: *Sometimes a headache is all in your head.* **RELAX.**

7. I love you!

It is important to love and to feel loved. To those who do not have loved ones, who lack a family, friends, or acquaintances, my advice is that you get out more, because every single one of us is looking for love. And I would ask those of us who are lucky, and have the good fortune of loving and being loved: When was the last time we said 'I love you' to our brother, sister, father, mother, grandfather, grandmother, or our best friends? They are only two words. Don't let time go by. It costs nothing.

Jose Ortega y Gasset said: *To love something is not simply 'to be', but rather to act towards that which is loved.*

8. Inhale, exhale

Isabel Arriagada (Aramadoma) states: *Breathing is an act which is deeply embedded in our cellular memory, is intuitive, and therefore intrinsically connected with survival.*

Breathing properly replenishes our physical health, increases mental capacity, and develops the spiritual aspect of our human and transcendent nature.

Rhythmic breathing helps us gain equilibrium and enhances the self-healing abilities within us; it helps us to overcome fear, negative emotions, and worry.

Those who breathe properly have less chance of becoming ill, and they generally have good circulation which allows them to be more resistant to changes in temperature. In addition, breathing strengthens the internal organs and muscles.

Practise breathing. Try breathing more slowly, with deep inhales and exhales, and see how it radically changes your emotional state.

There is a common circulation, a common breath. All things are connected. —Hippocrates

9. Hitting rock bottom

According to the magazine *Muy Interesante*, 121 million people in the world suffer from depression, a mental disorder that turns life into an ocean of sadness, discouragement, and hopelessness. In a recent study conducted by the *WHO* involving more than 24,000 people from 60 countries, it was concluded that between 9% and 23% of people affected by a chronic disease suffer depression in addition. These results, published in the British medical magazine the *Lancet*, also indicated that this combination is more detrimental to the psychiatric life than, for example, suffering from two or three chronic diseases simultaneously.

I consider myself a very optimistic person, regardless of what goes on in my life. Sometimes it has seemed as though I had hit rock bottom, but I have always thought that the only way to get ahead is to have a positive attitude, focus on the good things in life, learn all I can from people and events, and above all to surround myself with people who are open to life.

And that voice, that inner voice, is yours. Control your self-talk.

Every crisis contains a great opportunity for change. Only those who know how to see the positive can leverage the circumstances. —**Wally**

10. What do you think?

Jacinto Benavente wrote: *If people could hear our thoughts, very few of us would escape from being locked away as mad men.*

Did you know that 95% of our daily thoughts are derived from other older thoughts, and that by far the majority of them, depending on the individual, are negative? 95%!

Do you think about your thoughts? What type of voice do your thoughts have, and where do they come from?

It's interesting to pay attention to, and until you learn to do it, you cannot truly focus on what you are thinking.

Listen to your reflections. Modify the voice of your positive thoughts; make them more celestial, more divine, and more serious, giving them the tone of *'truth'*. And give the negative, inflammatory, and betraying thoughts an annoying and ridiculous voice. Try it!

What changes? What would happen if all your thoughts were positive?

Keep thinking about thinking and about thinking what you think. The key thing is to listen to and manage the voice of your thoughts. —**Bernardo Moya**

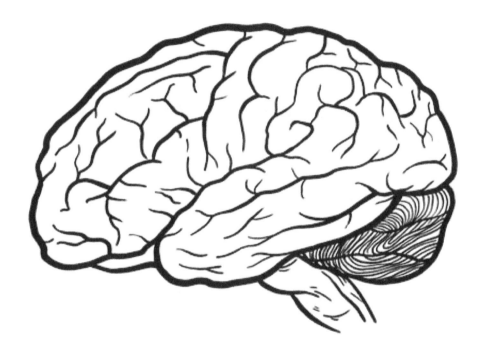

11. Curiosity

Regardless of youth, do you have a modern mentality, or are you anchored to the past and some of its taboos? What arouses your curiosity? What have you been planning to do for a long time? What are you waiting for? What would happen if your curiosity increased?

Today, begin to study, read, learn, or observe something that you are curious about. It's never too late.

Old age is the loss of curiosity. —**José Martinéz Ruiz (Azorín)**

12. Observe

Observe everything you see today—the blue sky, the intense green of the leaves, the shadows, the colour tones of the flowers, the rain, your loved ones, the colour of your children's eyes. Don't be blind.

I say: *Observe, because you can.* —**Bernardo Moya**

There are none so blind as those who will not see. —**Anonymous**

13. Be more charismatic

How can you have charisma?

Be more concerned about making others feel good about themselves than you are making them feel good about you. —Dan Reiland

It's true that some people are born with charisma; nonetheless, charisma is something that can be learned.

The secret consists of projecting self-confidence. Improve your posture, control your emotional state, adapt your body language to your manner of speech; practise in the mirror, take your time; think before speaking, speak with conviction; treat others the way you want to be treated, listen attentively, make people feel special.

My advice is to make eye contact, always greet people enthusiastically yet honestly, and above all: Listen.

14. Enjoy life

Abraham Lincoln said: *In the end, it's not the years in your life that count. It's the life in your years.*

Value yourself. Appreciate who you are, what you have, and those around you. Remember that we all have problems. Reaching goals is just a matter of perseverance. Try to always enjoy life.

Bernard le Bovier de Fontenelle said: *Don't take life too seriously; in any case, you won't come out of it alive.*

15. Seated or standing?

Who or what do you take for granted in your life? What do you count as a given? I'm not talking about something that is sitting in your living room ... I'm asking you if there's someone special in your life. Is there anyone who you are not valuing as much as they deserve? Can you think of someone?

Daniel Defoe wrote: *All our discontents about what we want ... spring from the want of thankfulness for what we have.*

16. Friendship

An Indian proverb says: *For the friendship of two, the patience of one is required.* **I see this as a great truth.**

A friend is one who may have been neglected, separated, and almost forgotten due to the circumstances of life, then reappears and within seconds you see a blossoming of that which you thought lost. That is a friend.

A friend will always be there when you need them.

Murcianika said: *A friend is a timely embrace and a word fitly spoken.*

A friend is ... something of incalculable value.

If you have real friends, act today and call them, arrange to meet up to eat, to go out, or simply to share your lives and experiences.

Benjamin Franklin said: *A brother may not be a friend, but a friend will always be a brother.*

And also: *Be slow in choosing a friend, slower in changing.*

17. Vices

Confucius said: *Vices are first fleeting, then guests, and finally masters.*

Do you have any vices? Determine today to get rid of one, however small it may be. Although I propose something different: Eliminate a big one, because if you are able to accomplish that, imagine what you are capable of.

18. Today towards tomorrow

Buddha said: *All that we are is the result of what we have thought. The mind is everything. What we think, we become.*

Based on this approach, what will you think about today? Today, what positive things will you dedicate time to? Remember, today will be a part of your future.

I say: *Think about what you are going to think about.* —Bernardo Moya

19. Silence

Manuel Azaña said: *If Spaniards spoke exclusively based on our knowledge, there would be a silence that would allow us to think.*

We also have the words of **Thomas Carlyle:** *Silence is the element in which great things fashion themselves.*

Georges Benjamin Clemenceau wrote: *It is more difficult to manage silence than words.*

Alexandre Dumas said: *For all evils there are two remedies: Time and silence.*

Try it. It's recommended, convenient, healthy, and great. Every day, for five minutes, alone, without anything or anybody, sit down and …

20. Change it up

The concept of *revolution* is defined as a radical and immediate change or transformation with respect to the recent past, which can be produced simultaneously in different spheres (social, economic, cultural, and religious, etc.). Revolutionary changes have far-reaching consequences and are often perceived as sudden and violent due to the fact that they make a break from the established order …

What revolution is pending for you? What will the 'new you' be like?

Aristotle said: *Revolutions are not about trifles, but spring from trifles.*

21. Read

Ralph Waldo Emerson said: *Many times the reading of a book has made the fortune of the man —has decided his way of life.*

Go out and buy a book, or order it on the Internet. DO IT TODAY!

22. Don't judge

Judge not, that you be not judged. For with the judgment you pronounce you will be judged, and with the measure you use it will be measured to you. —Jesus Christ

From now on, don't be prejudiced towards others. It is very easy to do, but, who are we to understand their circumstances? Do we know their motives? What is our opinion based upon? Our experience? Our values?

23. Give a hug

Amma (whose original name, Sudhamani, means 'jewel of ambrosia') was born to a humble family in the fishing town of Parayakadavu, in the district of Kerala, in 1953. She has devoted her life to *unconditional love*.

Considered to be a saint by her followers, it is estimated that Amma has embraced 25 million people in the course of her life, having transmitted to them a feeling of inner peace, acceptance or 'something indescribable', as one of them put it.

There is a great demand for her hugs, and she travels around the world to show people a little love. She is known to have embraced up to 50,000 people in a single day.

Although she is considered a saint, Amma does not embrace any specific religion. She only believes in the positive power of a hug, and the people who have had the good fortune to receive it—the lonely, the ill, the devout, or simply the curious—have experienced a sense of well-being and mystical elevation.

There are similar campaigns around the world and places where 'hug day' is celebrated. Without going as far as Amma, from now on, why not try to give more hugs and make them last a little longer.

To embrace and to kiss is to prepare the ground, and soon after follows the planting. —**Anonymous**

24. Today

Imagine that today was your last day at … (fill in the blank). For example: at your job, your house, with your friends, at …

What would you have to say and to whom? Write it down. It is an extraordinary feeling.

Seneca said: *As is a tale, so is life: not how long it is, but how good it is, is what matters.*

25. Losing weight

There's a simple way to lose weight, which has been practised by millions of people for ages: Eat what you need, eat good quality food, keep track of what you eat, and exercise.

Take control. How would you feel if you lost weight? Take responsibility for your own body. You can do it!

Staying slim is easy: you just need to develop an appetite for the things that you don't like. —Jane Russell

26. Time

Saint Augustine said: *What then is time? If no one asks me, I know what it is. If I wish to explain it to him who asks, I do not know.*

Manage your time. If necessary, and if it helps you think more clearly, take note of your daily and weekly activities. We all have the same amount of time: 24 hours a day, seven days a week.

Try this: instead of saying 'I don't know if I have time', say: 'I will find time'.

27. A worthwhile dinner

When was the last time you went out for dinner with your spouse? Have you gotten out of the habit over time? Don't make excuses. This should be *your time.*

***A slow dinner and a restful meal.* —Anonymous**

28. Maintain the flame

I never thought I would quote Bruce Lee on the subject of romance, yet I believe he describes love in an interesting way:

Love is like a friendship caught on fire. In the beginning a flame, very pretty, often hot and fierce, but still only light and flickering. As love grows older, our hearts mature and our love becomes as coals, deep-burning and unquenchable.

To maintain the flame, enhance the little things and make them lasting. Show your love. Buy flowers, pick a flower from the garden, leave a note, and pay attention to details. Express your love. But most importantly: demonstrate it.

29. Make memories

Make new memories; don't live off the old ones.

You may recall that in a previous passage I commented on how over 90% of our thoughts have previously passed through our minds. And that usually the majority of those are negative.

Make new memories the next time you feel your life is slipping by as you sit in the comfort of your couch watching movies and knowing you are missing out on the special times. MAKE MEMORIES.

Get up, go out, and discover new things with your family and loved ones.

Make new memories, take a risk, make a trip to some place you never imagined yourself going. Let your imagination fly. Create your own dreams. Live!

Our memories are the only Paradise from which we can never be expelled.
—**Jean Paul Ritcher**

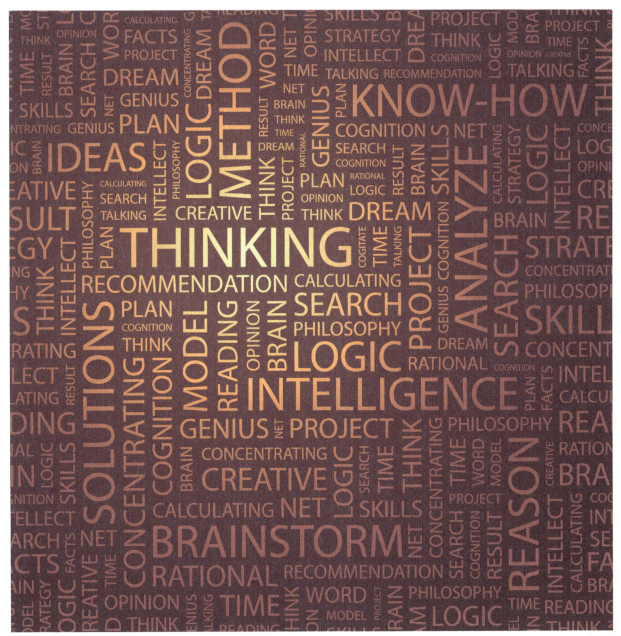

30. Spring in your step

Try the following today: as you walk, put a little spring in your step, and notice how by simply increasing your rhythm and pace, you will activate quicker thinking and improve your emotional state. You are likely to feel more energetic and dynamic.

The only way to be followed is to run faster than others. —**Francis Picabia**

31. You are an expert

You are the expert on yourself; there is no one in the world more knowledgeable about you. Analyse yourself objectively: What do you need to change, improve in, or do? Remember: Be objective. If you are not able to do that easily, try imagining that you hired someone (yourself, in this case) to analyse and evaluate you.

Write down the results of your research and act accordingly. You know your assignment. How will you improve? What will you do differently?

Joan Jimenez said: *An expert is someone who is fully aware of everything he ignores.*

32. Important

Often we're caught up in our daily lives, and we lose track of where we are going. We confuse what is important (now, today, and for tomorrow) with what is making us frazzled or stressed, with what is demanding our immediate attention. Learn to differentiate between important and urgent. Prioritise. Establish categories of priorities and allocate attention to your priorities. Plan your day, week, and month. Plan your entire year! What's important to you?

__Being prepared means much, being able to wait means more, but to make use of the right moment means everything.__ —Arthur Schnitzler

33. Smoke, smoke; die, die

Brooke Shields said: *Smoking kills. If you're killed, you've lost a very important part of your life.*

Create two lists. This might take you 20 minutes, but they could be the most important minutes of your life. First, make a list of all the people who would miss you if you were gone, and to what extent you think they'll miss you—and I'm referring to the things you truly believe they would miss. Next, make another list of all the things you wouldn't be able to do if your life was cut short. For someone who doesn't smoke, and wishes to apply this concept to another vice, go ahead. You know perfectly well which one I'm referring to. Yes, that.

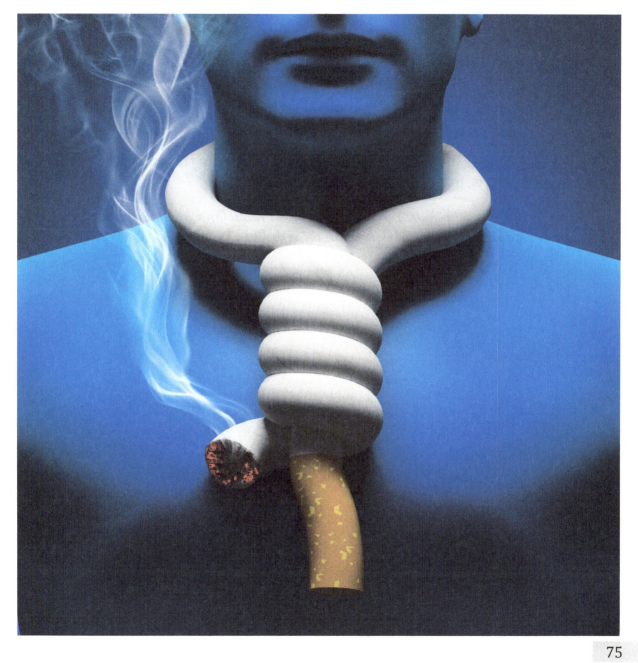

34. Observe your children

When they are young, our children imitate and observe what we do; they study our actions and our words. Today, follow their example and contemplate your children. Observe the love and purity of their actions, the way they watch television, how they play with their friends, their carefree ways ...

Sallust said: *When you return to your homeland at last, you'll discover it was not your old house you missed, but your childhood.*

35. Accept

Practise acceptance of events, circumstances, and your fellow travellers. You can't change the universe, and some things just happen, but think about the reasons behind things. What might the future hold for you? What can you learn from what happened? How can you benefit? What advantages could your difficulties provide? Live life, and accept it as it is.

Seneca said: *The willing, Destiny guides them; the unwilling, Destiny drags them.*

36. Be like water

In the face of adversity, difficulty, and problems, be like water.

Bruce Lee said: *Don't get set into one form, adapt it and build your own, and let it grow, be like water. Empty your mind, be formless, shapeless— like water. Now you put water in a cup, it becomes the cup; you put water into a bottle, it becomes the bottle; you put it in a teapot, it becomes the teapot. Now water can flow or it can crash. Be water, my friend.*

37. Inferior

Do you feel inferior to anyone? Or have you ever felt that way? We've all experienced a sense of inferiority to some degree at some point in our lives. Many people develop an inferiority complex, which makes them victims of themselves. It is a feeling derived from comparing oneself to others, considering it impossible to match up to them.

The truth is, there is no reason to feel inferior to anyone. Accept yourself just as you are, and become great at what you are.

Very successful, attractive, and charismatic people come in all types—they are overweight and thin, tall and short, of different races, of diverse origins, but always secure in who they are.

No one can make you feel inferior without your consent. —**Eleanor Roosevelt**

38. Forgive

Is there someone you need to forgive? You know who it is.

Pedro Calderon de la Barca said: *To overcome and forgive is to overcome twice.*

Alexander Pope said: *To err is human, to forgive divine.*

39. Weekend

Do something different. Plan a weekend with your loved ones. What's something you've wanted to do for a long time?

Variety is the spice of life. —**Anonymous**

40. Excuse me

It has been said that: *Coming up with excuses for failure is a national pastime.*

It's also said that: *Excuses are a way of letting others know how useless you are.*

There's nothing worse than listening to somebody make excuses for failure to fulfil their commitments. Don't justify yourself. How often do you make excuses instead of taking responsibility for your actions? Have you done it recently?

I say: *Excuse me, but excuses are inexcusable.* —Bernardo Moya

Man is born free, responsible and without excuses. —Jean Paul Sartre

41. Results

In life, there are only two types of people: those who make excuses, and those who achieve results. What type of person are you?

***The world demands results. Don't tell others of your birthing pains. Show them the child.* —Indira Gandhi**.

42. Are you silly?

Why not? Don't be so conventional! Don't take yourself too seriously. Break away from the norm and learn how to do something new, something you've never dared before. Don't be afraid of making mistakes and looking silly.

Ludwig Wittgenstein said: *If people never did silly things, nothing intelligent would ever get done.*

43. Copy

When we're young, we learn in school that we shouldn't copy others. In real life, it's really the opposite. It's always useful to learn from the more knowledgeable; those who are eloquent in their words, charismatic, educated, intelligent, charitable, athletic, funny, or skilful in the kitchen.

Therefore, begin today to copy those with skills and knowledge. Learn excellence!

***We are what we repeatedly do. Excellence, then, is not an act, but a habit.* —Aristotle**

44. Be useful

Winston Churchill said: *The problem with society today is that men don't want to be useful, but important.*

How can you be useful? Is there someone who needs you? How would they show their gratefulness for your help?

45. Visualise

Before you can see, you must visualise. —**Bernardo Moya**

Anything that was ever invented was first visualised. Devoting time to visualising what you want to achieve is very important. Spend time 'seeing yourself' in that new position, with your family, in your new home; picture yourself playing with your children, visualise yourself being happy and doing what you enjoy.

If you can see it, you can achieve it. —**Bernardo Moya**

46. Listen

Listen to others carefully, because in order to be understood, you must first learn to understand.

Nothing infuriates a charlatan as much as someone who is quiet and dignified. —Juan Ramon Jimenez, Spanish poet

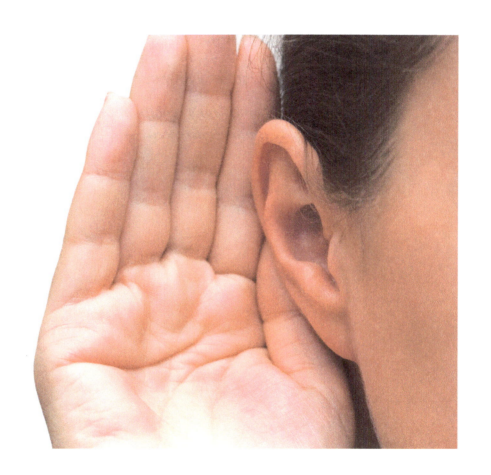

47. Conspiracy

Have you ever lost something and couldn't find it, and blamed some mysterious 'conspiracy'? Do you imagine that someone 'stole' your deodorant, your keys, or your favourite cup? Avoid thinking up conspiracies. Listen to your self-talk.

Someone once said: *Many explain historical events through conspiracies, but stupidity is underestimated.* —Anonymous

48. Accept and embrace criticism

Many of us are so immersed in our ego, in our 'ideal me', that we become incapable of seeing our 'real me'. Take a step back, and analyse what you really see in yourself.

Winston Churchill said: *Criticism may not be agreeable, but it is necessary.*

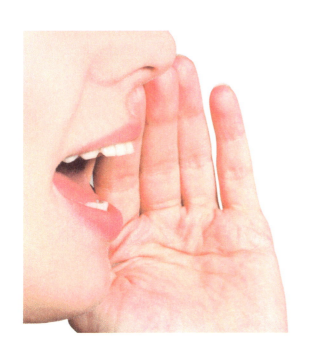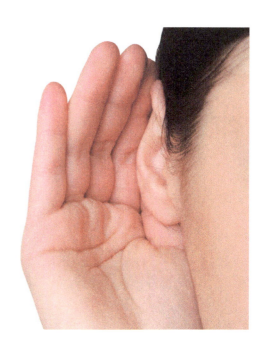

49. An optimistic but real future

Joaquin Sabina commented: *There is no worse nostalgia than to yearn for what never happened.*

If you haven't found your ideal partner or dream job, don't despair, because you still have time to find what you're seeking. Don't you think?

50. Young or old?

How old are you? Whatever your age, accept it. It's not your age but the attitude that you adopt toward life that matters most.

Pearl S. Buck said: *Enthusiasm is the daily bread of youth. Scepticism is daily ageing wine.*

51. Be generous

Be generous with everything: Your words, gestures, compliments, manners, deeds, and sharing what you have. When was the last time you showed generosity? Towards whom, and how? How would you feel if you were more generous? How would your generosity affect other people?

It has been said: *A man is sometimes more generous when he has but a little money than when he has plenty, perhaps for fear of being thought to have but little.* —Benjamin Franklin

52. What's your opinion?

What is your opinion of yourself? Do the opinions of other people matter to you?

How would you rate yourself? Be generous! There's always someone who has it worse than you. You are blessed, no doubt.

Do you get the idea? Value yourself—both what you are and what you have.

Seneca said: *What you think about yourself is much more important than what others think of you.*

53. Do you believe?

Do you believe in yourself? Think about it for a moment before you answer ...

You must believe in yourself to be successful in life. There is nothing you can't do if you believe in yourself.

How far can you go if you believe in yourself? How long would it take you?

Remind yourself often that you are better than you think you are.

Johann Wolfgang Von Goethe said: *It is a great error to take oneself for more than one is, or for less than one is worth.*

54. Can you imagine?

Are you imaginative? Do you take time to use your imagination? Through imagination we can accomplish two important things: Reconstruction of the past and anticipation of the future.

Richard Bandler, one of the creators of neuro-linguistic-programming, said: *The best thing about the past is that it's over. The best thing about the future is that it's yet to come. The best thing about the present is that it's here now.*

Although most of you understand this, how many of you apply it? Are you anchored to your past?

Anticipation of the future is the most creative aspect of imagination, and the most unique. Through anticipation we can imagine things, worlds, situations, and experiences we've never encountered. Anticipation rises above the here and now. It's not the past or the present that come to life, but the future.

Practise being less logical and more imaginative. Take your time. The more imaginative you are regarding what you want, the easier it will be to attain it.

Alfred Hitchcock said: *There is something more important than logic: The imagination.*

Albert Einstein offered: *Imagination is more important than knowledge.*

He also stated: *In times of crisis, imagination is more effective than intellect.*

55. Be resolute

The definition of resolution is as follows:

- Determination or decision to do something, for example: 'I have made a resolution to continue studying'.

- Vitality, courage.

Abraham Lincoln said: *Always bear in mind that your own resolution to succeed is more important than any one thing.*

What steps can you take to become more resolute?

56. Impatient?

Are you a bit impatient? Be patient ...

Life nowadays moves at a hectic pace. We eat, drink, and talk as though we barely had time to breathe. We wait impatiently for our computer to boot up in the morning or for the traffic light to turn green. Life nowadays is more like a sprint than a distance race.

__Patience is the strength of the weak and impatience the weakness of the strong.__ —Immanuel Kant

57. Do something different

If we keep doing what we're doing, we're going to keep getting what we're getting. —Stephen R. Covey

Do something different. Eat something different for breakfast, take a new route to work, read a different newspaper than usual or an article you would normally skip. Wear something you don't usually wear, change your glasses, or your haircut. Break up the monotony!

From today forward, could you do one thing differently every day?

How would it benefit you?

58. Happiness

There is only one way to happiness, and that is to cease worrying about things which are beyond the power of our will. —**Epictetus**

Are you happy without fully realising it? Would your life be considered 'ideal' in other parts of the world? Think about it.

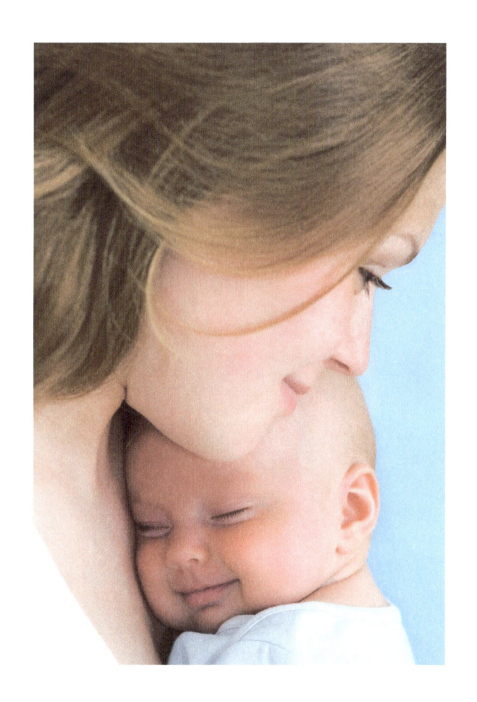

59. Measure your words

One word can change your relationship with a loved one for better or worse.

Measuring our words does not necessarily mean to sweeten their expression, but to foresee and accept their consequences. —**Abraham Lincoln**

How could you make your words kinder today?

60. What time do you have?

The question is ambiguous. You easily grasp the more obvious meaning, which is in regard to the hour indicated by your watch.

However, I am referring to the words spoken by **Benjamin Franklin:**

Since thou art not sure of a minute, throw not away an hour.

61. Make mistakes

In my life I have often been mistaken. I learned this quote at a very young age, and have referred to it innumerable times:

To err is human and to rectify is wise.

I also like the following: *There is no greater mistake than to have never been mistaken.*

Woody Allen says: *If you're not failing every now and again, it's a sign you're not doing anything very innovative.*

Don't be afraid of making mistakes. To err is human.

62. Be blind

Who would you naturally pay more attention to? A charming, handsome person who is physically fit and in their 30s or 40s? Or someone who is past 60, has grey hair, and is slightly overweight?

Without knowing your answer, I can imagine who you would feel more attracted to, but don't forget it's not about looks; it should be about the message and wisdom, the tone and rhythm of their voice.

My recommendation: when you meet new people, listen more attentively and pay less attention to what you see.

The eyes are useless to a blind brain. —**Arab Proverb**

63. Live life like a movie

There are many similarities between life and a movie.

You—the producer, and the scriptwriter—are responsible for everything. Whether the film of your life will become a blockbuster success or will never make it to the theatres depends on you.

Is your life a *comedy, romantic comedy, love story,* or an *action film*?

It's also up to you whether you watch it on a small screen or in a giant 3D theatre.

Life is a poorly edited movie. —**Fernando Trueba**

Do you agree with Fernando? Or is yours well-edited?

64. Adversity

Aristotle said: *Virtue is born of adversity.* **He also said:** *Education is an ornament in prosperity and a refuge in adversity.*

From his words I understand that in times of adversity we should be the ideal version of ourselves, the mast that supports the sail, the reference point, and the centre. Through adversity we learn, and your wisdom will depend on your ability to manage situations positively.

What have you learned from your adversities? How can you use them to your advantage in the future?

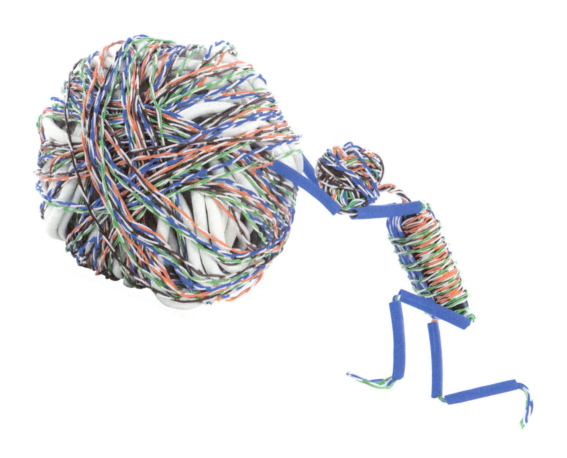

65. Your journey

Life is a journey—it has a departure and a destination. The vehicle in which you travel, your fellow journeyers, each incident, any detours or accidents you may encounter, are all part of the journey.

Keep in mind that every day is but a short trip within the great journey. I would suggest you roll down the window and put your head out; pull back the roof and enjoy the scenery.

Ralph Waldo Emerson said: *Life is a journey, not a destination.*

66. Plant a tree

Diego Andrade Dian said: *In the previous century, in order to leave your mark, you had to plant a tree, have a son, and write a book. In this century, to stand out you must plant a tree, have a son, and read at least one book in your lifetime.*

So ... when will you plant yours? Saturday or Sunday?

67. Want to succeed? Will to

This poem by Walter Dr. Christian Barnard has been an inspiration to me:

Thinking
If you think you are beaten, you are,
If you think you dare not, you don't,
If you'd like to win but you think you can't,
It is almost a cinch you won't.

If you think you'll lose, you've lost,
For out in the world we find,
Success begins with a fellow's will,
It's all in the state of mind.

If you think you're outclassed, you are,
You've got to think high to rise,
You've got to be sure of yourself before
You can ever win a prize.

Life's battles don't always go
To the stronger or faster man,
But soon or late the man who wins,
Is the man who thinks he can.

68. Teach - Help - Mentor - Inspire

Seneca said: *Long is the way of education through theories, short and effective by examples.*

They say the teacher appears when the student is ready.

Is there someone in your life who could benefit from your wisdom? Someone you could inspire?

Would their life change if you could help them? How would they thank you for it? How much satisfaction would it bring you to help them?

69. Minor flaw?

Jean de La Bruyere said: *Sometimes it is more difficult to remove a single defect than to acquire one hundred virtues.*

Recognise the flaws in yourself and take action accordingly.

Once you've improved on them, what kind of person will you become?

70. Envy somebody?

The Argentine writer Jorge Luis Borges said: *The topic of envy is very Spanish. The Spaniards are always having envious thoughts. To state that something is good, they say 'It is enviable'.*

However, I don't share his opinion. The way I see it, there is 'bad envy' and 'good envy'. I believe it *is* an enviable thing to be admired or looked up to.

Does that mean my life is 'ideal'?

Have only healthy envy. **As Napoleon Bonaparte said:** *Envy is a declaration of inferiority.*

71. Are you mediocre?

Are you mediocre?

Following is a definition of mediocrity:

· *Low or nearly bad quality.*

· *Lack of value or interest.*

· *Lack of intelligence or ability to accomplish something.*

Consider for a moment that you are a product at the supermarket, along with many other products around you. In other words, other men and women who also have arms, legs, a body, mind, etc.

Are you a mediocre product? Would you be in a highlighted area of the supermarket? Would you be on the eye-level shelves where everyone could see you, or would you be at ground level?

Or worse yet, would you be in the 'sales' area, or perhaps in the 'returns' pile?

Reinvent yourself, develop, and enhance your quality and presentation. Stand out in the ways you are outstanding.

As Honoré de Balzac said: *Mediocrity is not imitated.*

72. Developed?

In the previous passage I recommended developing.

During puberty, this concept is associated with a particular meaning. Over time I've come to understand that my life is in constant development. I try to evolve until the day I die. Because I'm not perfect, and I don't know everything, because there are a lot of places in the world I haven't been to. I have a lot yet to do and say!

The dictionary defines development as:

- *To cause to grow, increase, or progress.* Your mind*.

- *To carry out an idea or project.* Your life*.

- *Explaining a topic amply and in detail.* Every day*.

- *Carrying out all the operations needed in a mathematical calculation in order to find the solution.* Everything within your reach*.

*What I think development means:

*knowledge - knowing.

73. Doubt

Do you doubt someone or something? Have you ever experienced doubt? Exercise your ability to doubt—it's worthwhile. What are you doubtful of? Who *should* you be doubtful of?

Men become civilised not in proportion to their willingness to believe but in proportion to their readiness to doubt. —**Henry Louis Mencken**

We believe mainly because it is easier to believe than to doubt and faith is the sister of hope and charity. —**Alexandre Dumas**

74. What affects you?

Are you the kind of person who is affected by people, situations, or words?

It's not a matter of becoming insensitive, it's about understanding what affects you and how. If you're happy, yet you allow a moody individual to get you down, you're letting that person affect your feelings. As of today, take note of what affects you; but most of all, don't let it bring you down. If you feel displeased, think of someone you like, someone you love, something that makes you smile. Don't allow anyone or anything to affect your emotions.

Someone has said: *To handle yourself, use your head; to handle others, use your heart.*

75. Pictures on your wall

Recently Richard Bandler, the co-creator of neuro-linguistic programming (NLP), shared a perfect description of negative thinking.

If I came over to your house and painted a horribly ugly picture on your wall, what would you do? Would you leave it there where you'd have to see it every day? Or would you erase it by painting over it?

People allow ugly images to be "painted" in their minds, as a result of some unpleasant experience, or when someone hurts them. Then they look at and think about that horrible picture over and over again for years.

Do a calculation ... If you were to dedicate one hour a day to such thoughts, that would be 7 hours a week, 30 hours a month, 365 hours a year. Think for a minute: What you could do with those 365 hours?

How many walks could you take?
How many things could you do with your children?
How many books could you read?
How many jokes could you tell?
How many times could you make love?

Your mind can comprehend wonderful things. Don't waste your energy focusing on resentment and negative thoughts. —Anonymous

76. Habits

Think about your habits.

What bad habits do you have? Do you have productive habits? Do you have routines that have become habits?

Henry F. Amiel said: *Life is but a series of habits.*

Aristotle said: *To acquire certain habits from a young age is not a matter of little importance; it is of absolute importance.*

Once you've made your list, think about what habits could be interesting and beneficial for you. Do you believe you could eliminate your bad habits? How would that change you?

When we grow old, small habits become great tyrannies. **—Gustave Flaubert**

77. Knowing

We learn more in our first twelve years than in the rest of our lives. Our brain learns many daily activities early on, such as walking, talking, running, playing, jumping ... As we grow older, our ability to learn slows down and we acquire knowledge in a different way. When I was a boy, my father used to say that 'learning doesn't take up space'.

I recommend that you always study and learn. Read writings by those who inspire you; read biographies and academic works.

What would you like to learn? How would your life change as a result? And if you can learn something new, how many other new things could you learn?

To be aware of one's ignorance is a great step towards knowledge. —Benjamin Disraeli

78. Destiny

You probably wouldn't step into a taxi without knowing exactly where you want to go and how long it'll take you to get there. Why do so many people go through this world not knowing exactly who they want to be, or what they want out of life? The taxi (life) does not need to know, but the passenger (you) must know what the destination is (your objective). If you are not able to determine your objectives, life will happen without you realising it; you'll be lost —lost in the city, in your country, lost around people, and lost with yourself.

What is your destiny?

Vulgar spirits have no destiny. —**Plato**

79. Take a walk

Often when I feel worried or can't think clearly, I take a walk. It's difficult to describe what a 10- or 20- or 30-minute walk does. It helps you to think clearly and simplifies complex matters. Perhaps it has to do with the circulation and oxygen, or because it is time during which you are able to reason with yourself. In any case, it's highly recommended, and physically and mentally healthy. (By the way, let go of your digital world for just a moment —your tablet, iPod, etc. Just leave them home!)

__Morning fog, afternoon stroll.__ **—Anonymous**

80. Want to reach old age?

According to research done at Yale University, positive thinking lengthens life and is possibly just as important as exercising regularly or not smoking. A group of eight American psychologists discovered that people who spent their life thinking positively lived up to seven years longer than those who did not.

These studies, led by Doctor Becca Levy, have proven that positive thinking is just as important as having a good level of cholesterol or blood pressure. These people will live their last years with less worry, without remorse, and we can see it reflected in their lives.

Enthusiasm is contagious. It's difficult to remain neutral or indifferent in the presence of a positive thinker. —Denis Waitley

81. Time

This line from the movie *Faraway, So Close!* Provides an excellent definition of time:

Time is short. For the weasel, time is a weasel. For the hero, time is heroic. For the whore, time is just another trick. If you're gentle, your time is gentle. If you're in a hurry, time flies. Time is a servant, if you are its master. Time is your god, if you are its dog.

We are the creators of time, the victims of time, and the killers of time.

Time is timeless, you are the clock.

82. What shall we eat?

If you like the kitchen as much as I do, you'll understand my thoughts that follow. When I think about something appetising, first I 'see' or visualise it; then I mentally 'taste' it. I see the colours and think about the ingredients. I review my menu, and plan how to prepare each dish. I think about all the details—the texture, the flavour of freshly made food, the scent of coffee on the table. My salivary glands are activated and I feel ravenous.

For me, eating and cooking are a passion—a passion for flavour, aroma, texture, sweetness, colour, heat, and most of all, pleasure; the satisfaction of eating well.

Why not plan your day, week, year, or life in a similar way?

Visualise your coming day in detail: What will people think when they see you, when they interact with you, or shake hands with you? How will *you* feel? What ingredients will you need to use to make your 'perfect plate'? What could you go without? Permeate your life with colour, flavour, aroma, warmth, love, and sweetness. Enjoy and make it count.

Good food satisfies the senses before the belly. —**Anonymous**

83. Love yourself

Love and appreciate yourself. What can you do to value yourself more? Could you take better care of your mind and body?

He that falls in love with himself will have no rivals. —Benjamin Franklin

84. The ephemeral life

This is the story of an ephemeral insect that lives up to three years in water and one day in the air. The larva remains underwater for two or three years, and during that time lives an active life—hunting other insects for food, making houses in the sand or the mud, and slowly preparing itself for what is to come. Finally the great day arrives; the stage of the chrysalis has passed, and the insect climbs to the surface of the water in perfect condition to begin its flight, except that it is still wrapped in larval skin. When it manages to shed this, it is able to fly. This insect with transparent wings usually abounds in the warm months in canals, pools, and rivers. His life in the air never exceeds more than one day. Often no more than a few hours transpire between the time it leaves the water and the time it dies. In this short span of time, the female lays hundreds of eggs on the leaves of water plants, then its life ends. Its existence in the air has lasted only hours after having spent years in the water preparing ...

Life is bitter or sweet, it's long or short. What does it matter? He who enjoys it finds that it's short, he who suffers finds that it's long. —**Ramon de Campoamor**

85. Facial muscles

Facial muscles are known to be the most developed in the animal kingdom. Among other functions, facial muscles serve the purpose of creating the expressive movements by which we show fear, surprise, joy, doubt, etc. And most of them are found around the mouth … to give you an idea, when we kiss we move approximately 64 muscles. Put them to use.

It takes forty muscles to frown, but only fifteen muscles to smile. —**Swami Sivananda**

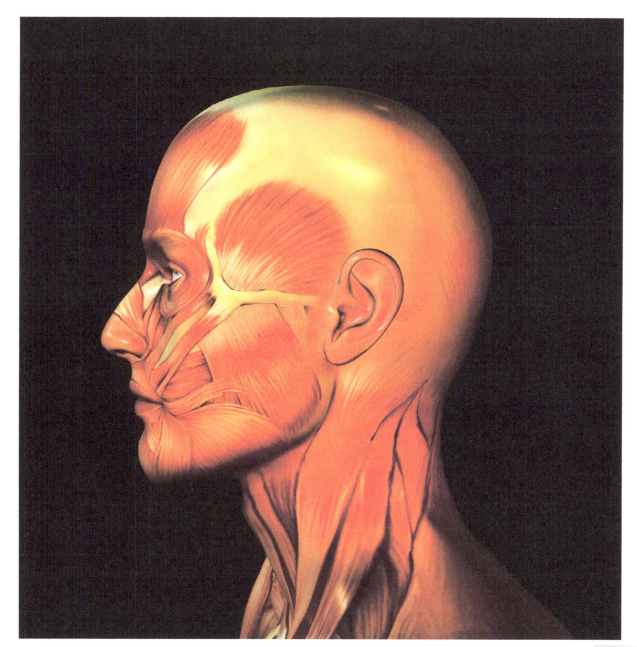

86. Have a laugh!

The benefits of laughter are evident and the specialists agree: it facilitates the movement of the diaphragm, increases lung capacity, improves breathing, strengthens the heart, aids digestion by making the liver vibrate, lowers hypertension, increasing circulation, and tones the muscles. In an outburst of laughter, the 400 facial muscles are nearly all activated, something that does not occur with a serious face.

Let me tell you a joke: *Two hunters from New Jersey are coming out of the forest when one of them collapses on the ground. It seems he's not breathing and his eyes are rolled back. His companion rushes to call the emergency services. With a broken up voice he tells the operator: 'My friend is dead! What should I do?' The operator answers slowly: 'Above all, be calm. I can help you. First, make sure he's dead.' There's a moment of silence, followed by a gunshot. The hunter who is talking to the emergency services says: 'Done. Now what?'*

At its core, having a sense of humour is keeping things in perspective.
—Antonio de Senillosa

87. 1% - 100%

I recently met a motivational speaker named Humphrey Walters. He dedicated the first part of his life to doing business, and the second part of his life to learning about excellence and leadership in sports. At the age of 58 he embarked on a sailboat race across the world, which took him 11 months to finish. He was the right hand of Clive Woodward, the UK manager whose team won the gold cup in rugby for the first time in 2003. He also works with the Chelsea soccer team and Formula 1 Virgin Racing team. He is the author of many quotations. I would choose the following as one of the most outstanding:

Winning or losing is a matter of inches and seconds.

To see the difference, he recommends doing things 1% better than they're usually done.

88. Beauty

Do you like pretty things? Confucius said:

Everything has its beauty, but not everyone sees it.

89. Manage your mind

In one of my books I used the metaphor of being the manager of your mind. You're in charge of your mind, your thoughts, what you see and feel. A manager's job is to direct, hire, train, and dismiss personnel (in this case, thoughts and attitudes) so that you can reach the end of the year with profits (a prosperous and happy life).

Plato said: *The human body is the carriage; the self, the driver, the thoughts, the reins; the feelings, the horses.*

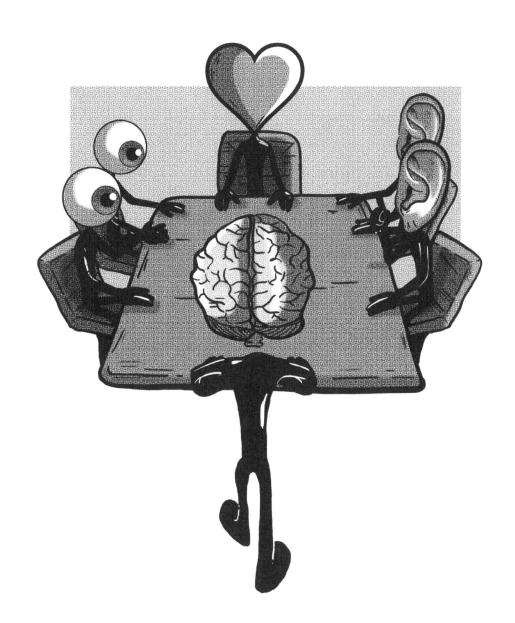

90. Grateful or ungrateful

Aesop stated: *Gratitude is the sign of noble souls.*

He also said: *Unworthy is the man who can receive a favour but cannot return it.*

Who should you be grateful to? How would they reward your gratitude?

Find reasons to be grateful. It's never too late.

91. Priorities

The concept of priority is described as follows:

- When a person or thing is more significant than another person or thing. To be or go first in time or place.

- That which must be cared for, considered, or done before other things.

- Greater importance, superiority.

In life we tend to overlook priorities (family, loved ones) until a serious event makes us aware of what we are doing. Who or what is high priority for you?

One should never forget that priorities are always priorities. —**Bernardo Moya**

92. Problems

How do you react to a problem?

For every problem there is a solution. Problems are a part of life.

People who choose to end their lives make a permanent decision based on a temporary problem.

When faced with a complicated situation or adversity, what's your reaction? Do you confront the problem? How do you confront it? Do you procrastinate until it's too late?

Next time you're faced with a problem you want to confront, try this:

Think about what will happen if you don't confront it. How will it affect the people involved? How will you feel? Will you end up being affected if you don't take the necessary steps?

Now, think about it as if you are being given a second chance. How will you deal with it differently? Who can you ask for help and advice? Think it through, compile a list, and act upon it.

A character is defined by the kinds of challenges he cannot walk away from. And by those he has walked away from that cause him remorse.
—Arthur Miller

93. More joy

Pearl S. Buck said: *Many people lose the small joys in the hope for the big happiness.*

Anatole France stated: *If we emphasised our joys as we do our sorrows, our problems would lose significance.*

What does joy mean to you? Who has shared joyful times with you? What can you do to have more satisfaction in your life? Write it down and do it.

94. Lost?

Have you ever been defeated? Have you ever lost?

Maybe the final result is actually the opposite—perhaps by losing you gained more in the long run. What did you learn from losing?

__Defeat has a positive side: it's never final. On the other hand, victory has a negative side: it's never final.__ —__José Saramago__

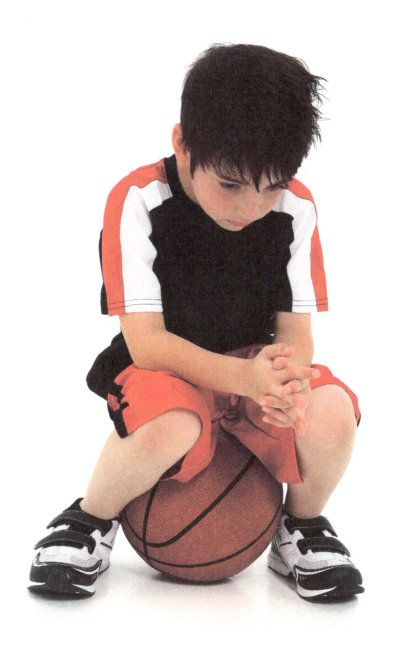

95. Be different

I'm not talking about being different from other people. I'm talking about trying something new, something you rarely do, that is out of your 'comfort zone'. Challenge yourself by trying new things —things you've never done and always wished you could do.

What would life be if we had no courage to attempt anything? —**Vincent van Gogh**

96. You will die

Keep that in mind, mainly so you can use your time wisely. What remains for you to do? What is something you need to do but have been postponing? Ask yourself, and then take action. Live!

Live as if you were going to die tomorrow. Learn as if you were going to live forever. —Analus de Insulis

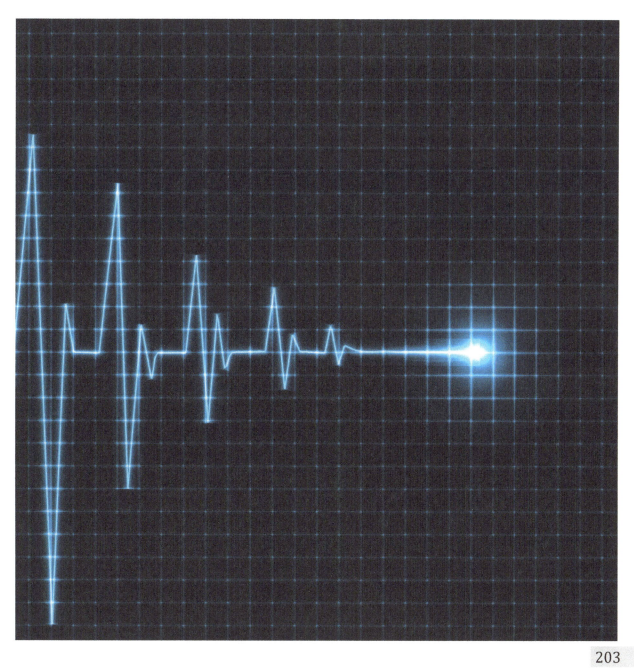

97. Plan. Schedule

If you want something to happen, schedule it. Plan your day the night before. Tell yourself: 'I'm going to wake up feeling dynamic, happy and in a good mood'. Picture in detail what your day will be like, the clothes you want to wear, and what you're going to do. You'll be surprised at how your life changes.

What are things in your life that you could plan or schedule?

Chance favours only the prepared mind. —Isaac Asimov

Chance favours only the programmed mind. —Bernardo Moya

98. Your next year

Don't wait for January 1st to start planning the year. Plan now. If you are like me, you have twelve months in a year, so plan every month. The way I see it, the first month represents more than merely a twelfth of the year; I believe that you can't go wrong by setting an ambitious first month. Once you've mapped out and written down your goals ... fulfil them!

What would your ideal year look like? What would you accomplish?

The Duke of Alba said: *A good general's objective is not the fight, but victory. He has fought enough if he achieves victory.*

Peter Bamm stated: *What matters in life are not the goals we set, but the paths we follow to achieve them.*

99. Listen

Brian Tracy said something in one of his audiobooks that really struck me: If you listened to an audio book for 90 minutes every day as you drive or commute, that time could account for a master's degree or other university degree.

I must admit I'm not a very fast reader, although I often read several books simultaneously. Audio books are ideal for me. The author *reads his work to me,* and I can assimilate a two hundred page book in only three or four hours!

***You have to study a great deal to know a little.* —Montesquieu**

100. If you were selling your life ...

Imagine that you have to 'sell your life'. In other words, imagine you're looking for a potential buyer to acquire your life as it is. You would have to present an articulate description of the most interesting aspects of yourself: your body, mind, family, loved ones; your future and plans. Try expressing that and writing it down.

Does that help you to value who you are and what you have? In what ways, and when, can you improve?

If any man, even an average man, knew how to describe his own life, he would write one of the greatest novels ever written. —**Giovanni Papini**

101. Meet - Communicate

For those in the business world, it's normal and convenient to get together with your supervisors and co-workers to discuss things such as sales, relations between employees, promotions taking place, and the financial state of the company.

When was the last time you discussed your relationship, your children, or your feelings with your spouse? Allot time to talk, analyse, and discuss (without arguing).

What society is more important than family society?

Ralph Waldo Emerson said: *Society begins when a man finds his partner.*

102. Find a coach

Rafael Nadal has a coach and Tiger Woods has a coach. The most outstanding people in any area have or have had a coach who trains, advises, and guides them. —Someone who provides an independent perspective on how to improve physically or mentally. Can you think of someone you admire and could get advice or coaching from? If you don't have anybody, there are experts who are willing to help. It's healthy and recommended and will cause you to grow as a person.

It's never the same to discover the truth for oneself as to hear it from someone else. —Aldous Huxley

Antoine de Rivarol said: *Reason consists of truths that must be spoken and truths that must be kept silent.*

I would say: *Reason consists of truths that must be spoken and truths that must be heard.* —Bernardo Moya

103. Your wealth

We tend to measure our wealth from a financial perspective. As I see it, that's not wealth. Wealth is my family and friends, my knowledge and experience. That's wealth to me.

Are you well-informed about your own value, heritage, and true wealth?

Can you help someone else to realise how wealthy or fortunate they are?

The greatest good you can do for another is not just share your riches, but to reveal to him his own. —**Benjamin Disraeli**

104. Inner smile

I imagine you've had days, like I have, where you wake up with a smile that you know comes from within, a feeling of inner joy that shows outwardly on your face.

With practice, this can become a daily experience.

Try it: smile inside and let that joy take over your body, starting at your stomach, going down to your toes; then let it rise up slowly through your legs, up to your chest and shoulders, until it reaches your head. Smile! As you smile, try some physical action, like touching your nose for example. Practice this throughout the day, and you'll start to notice how every time you touch your nose you start smiling.

A smile is a seed that grows in the heart and blooms on the lips. —Martha Stevenson

A smile happens in an instant but its memory can last a lifetime. —Anonymous

105. Practice

Practice is an exceptional teacher. —Pliny the Younger

Everything in life requires practice. Through practice we can turn something that seems very difficult and complex into something simple. Learning to drive or ride a bicycle for the first time is always difficult, as is learning a new sport. Practice is essential for anyone wanting to learn a new discipline. The first step is to observe and to practise in your mind, and then, carry it out.

I say: *Confidence precedes success, and practice precedes confidence.*
—**Bernardo Moya**

106 Rescue yourself

Tim Robbins said: *We are our own dragons as well as our own heroes, and we have to rescue ourselves from ourselves.*

Rescue yourself, because nobody is going to do it for you. It's not easy, but the sooner you face it the better. If you're hoping someone will knock at your door and offer you a job, a problem-free life, or a financial solution, I can tell you right now —and I wish I were wrong— that it's not going to happen.

So rescue yourself. Survive. Does the motto 'Find a life' ring true?

107. Limiting beliefs

Belief is when we feel certain about the meaning of something. It's a personal affirmation that we claim true.

Beliefs in many cases are subconscious; they affect our perception of others and ourselves, of things and situations.

Through our system of beliefs and values we give meaning and logic to our model of the world, to which we are deeply connected.

Beliefs are based on ideas, which we base on our personal experiences.

Beliefs can be empowering or limiting. Empowering beliefs boost our confidence in our own abilities, allowing us to face difficult situations successfully. Limiting beliefs steal our energy and make us unable to face certain situations.

We should question beliefs that limit us in reaching our goals and objectives.

Some limiting beliefs could be:

· Marriage is not for me.

· I must be rich to be happy.

· All men are self-centred.

Through coaching techniques and neuro-linguistic programming, you can work on overcoming beliefs which limit your behaviour.

I've known many people with limiting beliefs: phobias, fear of flying, aversion to spiders or small spaces. Their life was limited by their fears for many years; they were convinced that they could never overcome them.

Beliefs that affected their life and held them back were eliminated in a matter of minutes.

Once they overcame those beliefs, they all asked the same questions: What more am I capable of? What more can I overcome? Analyse the limiting beliefs in your life. And do something to get rid of them.

Franz Werfel stated: *For those who believe, no explanation is necessary; for those who do not believe, no explanation is possible.*

108. Empowering beliefs

At the beginning of 1954, the world of sports had never seen a human being run 1 kilometre and a half (one mile) in less than four minutes. It was essentially considered impossible. But the athlete Roger Bannister did it on May 6, 1954. In the next twelve months, at least six more athletes did the same.

The previous record had not been broken for nine years. Once it had been broken, 37 athletes surpassed it in a little over a year and over 300 athletes in two years. In 1999, the current record of 3.43.13 was set.

This was all because Bannister eliminated a limiting belief. It is a fact that impossible acts have become possible ...

What are your empowering beliefs? What do you believe you're capable of but haven't yet done?

You set the limits of your limits. —**Bernardo Moya**

They didn't know it was impossible, so they did it. —**Mark Twain**

109. Exaggerate

Exaggerating means:

To give excessive proportions to what is being said or done, to represent something as being larger, greater, or worse than it really is.

They say we Andalusians exaggerate, and our jokes and humour are filled with exaggerations. I believe it's very characteristic of Spaniards; and I like it.

You should try it and see how people react. Exaggerate! Exaggerate a kiss or a hug when greeting a loved one. Exaggerate when greeting people in the morning at work—you'll likely see that people react positively.

For example: *Hey Fernando! How are you? Good morning!*

What do you feel when you hear something like that?

Antonio Machado said: *In love a little exaggeration feels right.*

Anatole France stated: *If we emphasised our joys as we do our sorrows, our problems would lose significance.*

110. It depends on your point of view

Have you thought about the meaning of the oft-used phrase 'it depends on your point of view'? Even problems can affect you very differently depending on your perspective.

If you're in the middle of a difficult situation, it's best not to take it too intensely; try to distance yourself from it a bit. If you're mentally viewing the problem with yourself 'inside of it', you won't be able to think objectively.

Next time you deal with a problem or concern, try viewing it from an outside perspective, as if you were not part of or within the problem. Notice how you observe it. Has your viewpoint changed? Does it seem less intense?

If there is any one secret of success, it lies in the ability to get the other person's point of view and see things from that person's angle as well as from your own. —**Henry Ford**

111. Motivation

The word 'motivation' covers a process which is the result of an interaction between my 'self' and my surroundings; between my attitudes and my view of the world, and the outside world. That process always starts with me (my inner motivation), but depends on what exists around me (my outside motivation). That process is neither fully external nor fully internal; it's a result of the relationship between both.

I see motivation as the 'fuel' for life. Whatever you're going to do, you need fuel. Motivation is vital to anything you wish to accomplish in life.

If you were highly motivated in any of your activities, what would that feel like? How would you be better prepared to handle any situation?

People often say motivation doesn't last. Well, neither does bathing—that's why we recommend it daily. —Zig Ziglar (author and lecturer)

112. Act

To act means 'to take steps'.

The difference between a person who is successful and one who is not is that the first creates cohesion between speaking and acting. He dreams, because dreams are part of the process of getting new ideas and solutions, and he also wakes up from his dreams and finds a way to make his vision or objective a reality.

We all feel comfortable in familiar settings. Successful and confident people understand that despite seeming uncomfortable, unfamiliar settings often cause us to grow as individuals. It's the uncertainty that brings fulfilment in life.

We should all aim for such cohesion and be on the right side of that difference. Find a way to carry your projects to completion; fight for them.

Thomas Carlyle said: *Doubt, of whatever kind, can be ended by action alone.*

Aesop wrote: *All speech is vain and empty unless it be accompanied by action.*

A Chinese proverb says: *Great souls have wills; feeble ones have only wishes.*

113. Make plans

There is a widespread story in personal development circles telling how a survey done at a top ranking university (sometimes Harvard is named, sometimes Yale) during either the 1950s or 1970s revealed that only 3% of students wrote out their goals. The story goes on to say that when the students who filled in the survey were approached 25 years later, the same 3% had nearly all gone on to reach their goals, and live successful lives, while the rest had not.

Although the survey has been cited by gurus and business motivators all over the world, in truth no such survey was carried out.

Nevertheless, the urban legend persists. If anything, it tells us that instinctively people really *want* it to be true. But no-one had thought to actually put it to the test in the real world.

In 2008, Dominican University rose to the challenge and tested groups with five different methods of goal setting. They were:

- Simply thinking about desired goals to be accomplished over the next 4 weeks
- Writing goals on an online survey
- Writing goals and then formulating commitments to act
- Writing goals, and sending the commitments to act to a supportive friend.
- Doing everything in 4, and then sending a weekly progress report to a supportive friend.

In every case, there was an improvement in how much was accomplished compared to simply thinking about doing it.

So the message is clear - it's not only about writing your goals down (as the mythical Harvard survey supposedly showed) but accountability and support really help you get things done.

Plan your life. Someone I know used to say that people spend more time planning holiday trips than they spend planning their future.

How would your life improve if you started planning it now?

__Good plans shape good decisions. That's why good planning helps us to make elusive dreams come true.__ —**Lester R. Bittel**

114. Crisis

Álex Rovira, in his book *La Buena Crisis (Good Crisis),* brings out the benefits of a crisis. In his book the author speaks of r-evolution, of transformation, of how times of crisis allow us to grow as individuals. They lead us to new horizons that force us to reinvent ourselves, or leave a part of who we are behind, to be born into something new.

Rovira explains how in Mandarin, the word 'crisis' means 'new unexpected scenario or opportunity'.

As Sigmund Freud said (quoted by Rovira): *I've been a lucky man in life; nothing was easy for me.*

115. Think about a loved one daily

Has it ever occurred to you that you could be a better father, mother, brother, sister, son, or daughter?

Love is to be shown by actions—a warm hug, a passionate kiss, a wink, or a compliment. Give a book as a gift; send an e-card or even a text message. It's simple; don't make it complicated.

True love is known not by what it demands, but by what it offers. —Jacinto Benavente

116. Fatherly love

My son sent me a YouTube link about a father and his son. They are known as 'Team Hoyt'.

The son, who was born with cerebral palsy and cannot move, walk, or do any activity on his own, was not able to communicate until he was 12. The father discovered that his son loved sports, and so as to do something together, they began to train and compete in races and even marathons. Since 1977 they have participated in over 1,000 competitions, including more than 200 triathlons, six of which were Ironman competitions. These consist of a 3.86 km (2.4-mile) swim, a 180.25 km (112-mile) bicycle ride and a marathon 42.2 km (26.2-mile) run, immediately after one another. In all of them, the father, who is now over 70, pushes his now 47-year-old son on his bicycle, in a chair when he runs, and pulls him in a boat when he swims.

When I watched the video I couldn't hold back the tears and think about what little I have done with my kids compared to this man, who possesses such a big heart.

It's never too late if you mean well. —**Anonymous**

It is easier for a father to have children than for children to have a real father. —**John XXIII**

We learn to love not by finding a perfect person, but by learning to see an imperfect person perfectly. —**Sam Keen**

(Find out more about the story by looking up 'Fatherly Love' or 'Team Hoyt'.)

117. Think 'Harry Potter'

J.K. Rowling, the author of the hugely successful *Harry Potter* series, did not have an easy life. Her mother died young, she had several failed marriages, and she never found a stable job. When she wrote the first of the *Harry Potter* books, eight publishers refused it. When it was finally published, she received just 2,000 Euros as a down payment, which she gladly accepted due to her financial struggle. Later ... her works have been translated into 65 languages and over 350 million copies have been sold.

I ask you, might you have a *Harry Potter* within you?

The people who get on in this world are the people who get up and look for the circumstances they want, and if they can't find them, make them. —**George Bernard Shaw**.

Talent alone cannot make a writer. There must be a man behind the book. —**Ralph Waldo Emerson**

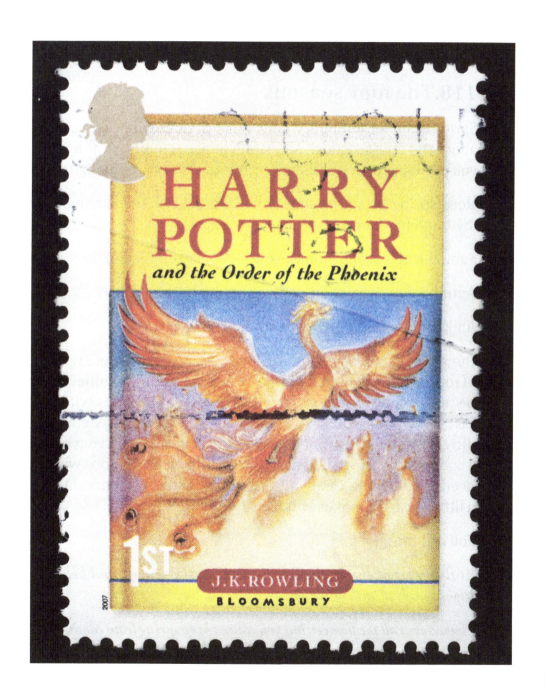

118. The four seasons

Spring, summer, autumn, winter. What comes to mind when you think about the four seasons? Allow one image to enter your mind when you pronounce each of them: spring ... summer ... autumn ... winter ...

Does spring bring to mind flowers, greenery, the singing of birds, love, and fresh morning air?

Summer: the beach, humidity, vacations, and family?

Autumn: windswept leaves, rain, going back to work?

And winter: cold, storms, coats, and chimneys?

Our days, weeks, and lives also have four seasons. There will be days of total spring, days that will seem like summer, and others that will be pure winter. Some days will have all four seasons within them. Just remember: you're the sun in your planetary system, and you dictate the distance from your sun, and choose your favourite season. There will be times when you would like a little more warmth, or need some rain to clean out the atmosphere, and other days where a little fresh air makes you feel alive.

You call the shots.

At the heart of every winter lives a pulsating spring, and behind every night comes a smiling dawn. —**Khalil Gibran**

You may cut all the flowers, but you cannot keep spring from coming. —**Pablo Neruda**

119. What would you do?

Picture waking up tomorrow and being able to do whatever you wanted, having all the time and resources in the world, no family problems; and most of all, imagine you could achieve anything because you have no fear.

What would you do? Where would you do it? What would you be like?

No one ever reached the top accompanied by fear. —**Publilius Syrus**

120. Don't lie to yourself

You know perfectly well what is right for you. You know innately what you need to do. You can see the 'ideal you' in your mind. So be true to yourself; don't lie to yourself, don't allow yourself to fail yourself.

A lie never lives to be old. —**Sophocles**

121. Resilience

Nature has a fast and convincing way of demonstrating its strength and our insignificance. Tremendous earthquakes, tsunamis, hurricanes, and floods seem to be occurring more frequently over time. These extreme situations can bring us down or make us stronger.

Positive psychology considers problems to be challenges that people face and overcome due to resilience.

Resilience is the ability of a person or group to recover and move on in the face of adversity. Sometimes difficult circumstances or traumas allow for the development of resources which were present all along but come to life in the face of an alarming situation.

Resilience is also a scientific term used in engineering to express the ability of an object to return to its original form after being submitted to great pressure.

In psychology, resilience is known as the ability of a person to overcome traumatic events and keep going with their lives.

Adversity has the effect of eliciting talents which in prosperous circumstances would have lain dormant. —**Horace**

122. Be a winner

Be a winner.

Vince Lombardi is considered one of the best American football coaches in NFL history. He led the Green Bay Packers to win five world championships within seven years.

His outstanding abilities were: discipline, work ethic, tough-mindedness, perseverance, commitment to excellence, fight, and above all: a winning attitude.

The following quote intelligently summarises the importance of our thoughts about who we are and about our character.

Winning is a habit. Watch your thoughts, they become your beliefs. Watch your beliefs, they become your words. Watch your words, they become your actions. Watch your actions, they become your habits. Watch your habits, they become your character.

He also said: *If it doesn't matter who wins or loses, then why do they keep score?*

123. The objective

The objective of the soccer player is to score goals; for the businessman, it's making money; for the musician, it's creating music; for the writer, it is to write. Everything has an objective.

What is your objective? Do you have personal or family objectives?

If you don't, what are you waiting for? Write a list with clear objectives as well as timeframes for when you plan on fulfilling them.

Objectives are the ingredients that bring purpose into our lives. —**Anonymous**

Keep targeting your target. —**Bernardo Moya**

Thank you for sharing your dreams with me!

I would like to thank you for reading this book. I hope you have found my tips and suggestions useful —and that along the way you've discovered new ways of looking at life to help you get the life you want and the very best from yourself.

Best Wishes,

Bernardo Moya

For more information on products, books and services I offer, please follow these links and addresses:

www.bernardomoya.com
www.thebestyouediciones.co
www.thebestyou.co
www.123formasdeverlavida.com
www.masconfianza.es
www.masmotivacion.es
www.youtube.com/user/bernardomoya64

The Best You Corporation Limited
Phone Number: **+34 911899594** (Spain)
                            +44 02079276502 (UK)
info@thebestyou.co
3rd. Floor, 5 Percy Street
London
W1T 1DG

Lightning Source UK Ltd.
Milton Keynes UK
UKOW07f1816110515

251293UK00001B/1/P

ESV - English Standard Version (ESV). Scriptures marked ESV are taken from the THE HOLY BIBLE, ENGLISH STANDARD VERSION (ESV): Scriptures taken from THE HOLY BIBLE, ENGLISH STANDARD VERSION ® Copyright© 2001 by Crossway, a publishing ministry of Good News Publishers. Used by permission.

GNT - Good News Translation (GNT). Good News Translation® (Today's English Version, Second Edition) Copyright © 1992 American Bible Society. All rights reserved.

KJV - King James Version (KJV). Scriptures marked KJV are taken from the KING JAMES VERSION (KJV): KING JAMES VERSION, public domain.

NASB - New American Standard Bible (NASB). NEW AMERICAN STANDARD BIBLE Copyright (C) 1960, 1962, 1963, 1968, 1971, 1972, 1973, 1975, 1977,1995 by The Lockman Foundation, a corporation not for profit, La Habra, CA. All rights Reserved

NET - New English Translation (NET). The Net Bible®, New English Translation copyright © 1996 By Biblical Studies Press, L.L.C. NET Bible® Its a registered trademark The Net Bible® logo, service mark copyright © 1997 by Biblical Studies Press, L.L.C. All rights reserved.

NIV - New International Version (NIV). Scripture quotations marked (NIV) are taken from the Holy Bible, New International Version®, NIV®. Copyright © 1973, 1978, 1984, 2011 by Biblica, Inc.™

NKJV - New King James Version (NKJV). Scripture taken from the New King James Version®. Copyright © 1982 by Thomas Nelson. Used by permission. All rights reserved.

NLT - New Living Translation (NLT). Scriptures marked NLT are taken from the HOLY BIBLE, NEW LIVING TRANSLATION (NLT): Scriptures taken from the HOLY BIBLE, NEW LIVING TRANSLATION, Copyright© 1996, 2004, 2007 by Tyndale House Foundation. Used by permission of Tyndale House Publishers, Inc., Carol Stream, Illinois 60188. All rights reserved. Used by permission.

TLB - The Living Bible (TLB). Scriptures marked TLB are taken from the THE LIVING BIBLE (TLB): Scripture taken from THE LIVING BIBLE copyright© 1971. Used by permission of Tyndale House Publishers, Inc., Carol Stream, Illinois 60188. All rights reserved.

06
FOREWORD

10
INTRODUCTION

16
PREFACE
Created to crave

32
CHAPTER ONE
Porn is in the eye of the beholder

56
CHAPTER TWO
Porn on the brain

82
CHAPTER THREE
Facing the truth

110
CHAPTER FOUR
Understanding the cycle of addiction

136
CHAPTER FIVE
Finding freedom

170
CHAPTER SIX
Porn widows & widowers

198
CHAPTER SEVEN
Further help, advice & resources

220
APPENDIX
A note for leaders

226
APPENDIX
Naked Truth & Care

FOREWORD

by Ian Henderson

One of the most famous stories found in Scripture is the parable of the prodigal son (Luke 15:11-32). A story of forgotten identity, unwise choices and outrageous forgiveness. Since Jesus first told this parable, multiple sermons have been crafted and preached on the son's folly, the brother's religious and hard heart and, of course, the father's love.

The turning point in the story is when the son hits rock bottom, 'comes to his senses' and decides to return home. At this point, the parable cuts to the happy and unexpected ending. The breathless sprint of a respectable man. A close embrace of a father and his lost child. A celebration of restored relationships and new beginnings.

On that day, the son's fear, doubt and shame are replaced with forgiveness, dignity and hope.

This story is a story of hope. Regardless of how messed up we have become or how far we have travelled from our Father's home, God does not forget who we are. We are His children and He is always waiting for us with an embrace and an offer of new life.

Let me say that again.

There is hope. It does not have to be like this.

You don't have to eat pig swill! You can return!

This book serves as a practical guide for the journey home.

Every mile that the son had travelled to pursue pleasure needed to be retraced. Sometimes I wonder about that journey between the pigsty and his father's home. How long did it take? Were there dangerous roads with bandits, steep hills and rivers to traverse?

The journey between addiction and freedom is a retracing of the miles walked away from our Father's house. Every journey is different and it can take time to return home.

Paula Hall's years' of experience means she has made this journey many times with many people. She knows the potential dangers and the bandits' hiding places. She knows that there are times when the road gets steep and extra effort is needed. She knows that further down the wide and rushing river, there's a bridge. In other words, this book has been written by someone who knows the way.

As you walk along the path back to your Father, this book is a necessary tool to carry with you. Meditate on the Scriptures, engage with the reflections and scribble notes. Make this the field guide to your personal recovery.

If you are reading this book because you struggle with porn, or because you love someone who struggles, my hope is that you'll find a practical path to the Father, freedom and new life.

IAN HENDERSON
Founder of Naked Truth & Visible Ministries.

INTRODUCTION

"Confronting Porn" is a practical self-help book, written for Christians who are troubled by their use of pornography. It is also designed for partners, pastoral carers and professionals seeking to support them.

The problems associated with pornography addiction are on the increase. High-speed internet porn is accessible and available anywhere and everywhere. And Christians are not immune from becoming trapped. In fact, porn and sex addiction is estimated to affect up to 50% of Christians. Judging by the increasing number of enquiries to services such as the 'Naked Truth Project' and our Christian recovery services at 'Paula Hall & Associates,' the problem is growing.

Porn and sex addiction affect both Christian men and women. It includes those who are new to faith and those who would describe themselves as knowing Christ from the earliest age. Many people have come to faith precisely because of their history of compulsive pornography use or sexual behaviours. We are seeing people who have sought solace and redemption in Christ - and have found it. But regrettably, like so many of humanity's problems, it sometimes requires more than prayer and faith to resolve these problems.

Throughout the pages of this book, you'll find practical, researched information and resources for understanding and beating sex and porn addiction. You will also find invitations to read Scripture and reflect in prayer on God's plan for your sex life. You will also read the candid stories of other Christian men and women who have fought against this addiction and who now carry the banner of hope and freedom.

This book has been written to be read in order, but if you're like me, you will skip to the chapters that seem most relevant and urgent to the situation you find yourself in now. And so, below, is an overview of what is in each chapter to help you find what you're looking for:

The Preface explains my viewpoint on addiction, and particularly on porn and sex addiction. There, I suggest that God created us to yearn for union with Him and addictions are a failed and misguided attempt to alleviate suffering and achieve peace.

Chapter 1 explores pornography in our current world and considers what healthy sexuality might mean for Christians today.

Chapter 2 is all about the neuroscience of addiction and explains why and how addiction happens and why so many are now getting hooked on internet porn.

Chapters 3, 4 and 5 are devoted to understanding porn addiction in more depth and provide information and questions for assessing if someone is 'addicted' and what the cause of it might be. There are also strategies for overcoming addiction and establishing a lifestyle of recovery.

Chapter 6 is written to help if you're a partner of someone who views pornography, whether that's occasionally, or compulsively.

Chapter 7 contains a list of books and online resources for further help and guidance and also additional spiritual exercises to help in recovery. You will also find a section listing Bible verses that will help you.

So finally, I hope and pray that this book will be a valuable resource to you, whoever you are and whatever circumstances you find yourself in. It has been a true blessing to me to write it and I pray that it will be a blessing to you, also.

PAULA HALL

PREFACE

Who is this book for?

First and foremost, I have written this to be a practical book. It will help anyone struggling with the impact of pornography - whether they would describe themselves as 'addicted' to porn, or just someone trying to keep the temptation at bay. This book is for them.

If you are a partner of someone who uses porn and you don't know how to respond and react, this book is for you too.

This book is also for people in ministry of any kind who want to think more about the role of pornography in culture today and in particular, how it impacts the Church.

It is also for Christians everywhere who want to help others whose lives have been damaged by pornography or sex addiction.

Before launching into Chapter One, and the main content of the book, I want to give an outline of my views on desire and sexuality as a Christian. I also want to explain how I view the problem of addiction, particularly sex and porn addiction, from both an academic and a spiritual perspective. I hope this will provide a context within which readers can make sense of what I'm saying and reflect on their own spiritual viewpoint.

Please be aware that I am not a theologian and that I

am writing from my own personal experience and exploration. It may not reflect all denominational views and doctrines, but my hope is that it will encompass most. You may not agree with my perspective, and that is fine. I'm not saying it's the right one, and certainly not that it's God's view, but before we can fully address a problem, we need, at least, to have some understanding of what we believe it is.

Created to crave?

Why did God create us?
To worship Him? To serve Him? To obey Him?

The answer is, of course, "Yes" - as all of these reasons are clearly stated in the Bible. But God does not need us to run His world, nor to prop up His ego. There are numerous writings in the Bible indicating that we were created to love Him. If we love God, as we are commanded to, then we will want to obey, serve and worship Him. But I believe He offers us so much more than that.

One of my favorite Christian writings of all time is a paraphrase of the First Principle and Foundation used in Ignatian spirituality. It begins:

> *"Lord, my God, when your love spilled over into creation, you thought of me. I am from love, of love, for love."*

I believe that God created us 'for' love, rather than 'to' love. We were created 'from' His abundant love and to 'share' His abundant love - to the point that we overflow in praise for Him and love for others. If you follow the metaphor of God the Father, then, like any parent who wants a child, you create one because you have love to give. Your hope for your child is that they will love you too. But more than that, your deepest desire is that your child will be happy.

Much has been written about why we were created and for what purpose, but the writers that have influenced me most and helped me understand the human spirit's deep hunger for happiness, are those who support the principles of Christian Hedonism. A number of Christian writers support the idea that man's fundamental purpose in life is to seek happiness. Blaise Pascal, a Christian philosopher writing in the 1600s said:

> *"All men seek happiness. This is without exception. Whatever different means they employ, they all tend to this end. The cause of some going to war, and of others avoiding it, is the same desire in both, attended with different views. The will never takes the least step but to this object. This is the motive of every action of every man, even of those who hang themselves."*

In my years as a psychotherapist, I have found this to be undoubtedly true. It seems that we spend our whole existence longing to escape pain - physical, emotional and psychological - and crave pleasure. All my clients want to feel better. They seek respite from their pain and a solution to their unhappiness. Furthermore, they want to know how to be happy – and stay happy.

Over recent years there has been a growth in one particular field of psychology known as "Positive Psychology." It endorses and encourages therapists to spend less time exploring why clients may be unhappy, but rather focus on what makes them happy. Martin Seligman, one of the key influencers in the field, discovered after extensive research that the people who are happiest in this life are those who lead a 'Meaningful Life'. He describes this as a life that finds fulfillment in living for a purpose greater than oneself. As Christians, this should not surprise us. The Bible, and particularly the Psalms are full of promises of the abundant joy we can find in our relationship with God. Indeed as a Christian, I believe there is no greater happiness than the pleasure we can find in God. The quest for the joy that only He can bring, is indelibly written on our souls. St Augustine said:

> *"You have made us for yourself and our heart is restless until it rests in you."*

The Bible often uses the language of thirst and hunger - primal survival needs - that only God can truly satisfy.

> *"As the deer pants for water, so I long for you, O God. I thirst for God, the living God." (Psalm 42:1-2 TLB)*

> *"My soul thirsts for You, my flesh yearns for You, In a dry and weary land where there is no water." (Psalm 63:1 NASB)*

> *"Blessed are those who hunger and thirst for righteousness for they will be filled." (Matthew 5:6 NKJV)*

> *"Jesus stood and said in a loud voice, 'If anyone is thirsty, let him come to me and drink. Whoever believes in me, as the Scripture said, streams of living water will flow from him.'" (John 7:37 NASB)*

> *"I am the Alpha and the Omega –the Beginning and the End. To all who are thirsty I will give freely from the springs of the water of life." (Revelation 21:6 NLT)*

God created us to crave the joy that only He can provide. He promised us the 'desires of our heart' and, whether we're a believer or not, somewhere deep in our DNA is an inbuilt craving for His promises. But we crave not just happiness, but ecstasy. We want a transcendent, euphoric state that lifts us above the trials of this world and creates a sense of deep inner peace and communion with something greater than ourselves.

And we yearn to find someone who can truly know us, whom we can depend on and trust to meet our deepest needs. Perhaps we will never achieve it in this life, but that doesn't stop us yearning for it and feeling pain when we are separated from it. If you believe that we were created to crave, then we are all addicts – to a lesser or greater extent. The question is, what are we addicted to? Is it God and having more and more of Him, or is it another source of solace and ecstasy? Regrettably, many of us look for what God promises in all the wrong places. Perhaps this constant search for fulfilment in things that won't satisfy is one of the Devil's most cunning plans.

In C S Lewis's 'The Screwtape Letters', the elder demon instructs his nephew, the junior tempter, in the following way:

> *"Never forget that when we are dealing with any pleasure in its healthy and normal and satisfying form, we are, in a sense, on the Enemy's ground. I know we have won many a soul through pleasure. All the same, it is His invention, not ours. He made the pleasures: all our research so far has not enabled us to produce one. All we can do is to encourage humans to take the pleasures which our Enemy has produced, at times, or in ways, or in degrees, which He has forbidden. Hence we always try to work away from the natural condition of any pleasure to that in which it is least natural, least redolent of its Maker, and least pleasurable. An ever-increasing craving for an ever diminishing pleasure is the formula.... To get the man's soul and give nothing in return–that is what really gladdens Our Father's heart."*

As you will see as you continue to read through this book, 'an ever increasing craving for an ever diminishing pleasure' is an almost perfect definition of addiction.

What is addiction?

Addiction then is defined by craving. It is about our hunger and our thirst. If you are an addict, whether that's an alcoholic, drug addict or sex addict – you don't just 'fancy' another fix, you crave it. And make no mistake, craving is psychological hell. It can dominate your every moment, wake you up in the middle of the night and invade your dreams when you sleep. Craving can blot out everything that's good in your life so that all you can think about is a way of ending the pain of craving. Whatever the object of your addiction, ultimately the desire is more about ending the craving than enjoying your drug of choice. When people are dismissive about addiction and say that it's 'just a choice' and that people should exert more willpower, they simply don't understand the power of craving. It's true that people do ultimately choose their behaviour, but they can't choose not to crave. Gerald May in his book 'Addiction and Grace,' says:

> *"Willpower and resolution come and go, but the addictive process never sleeps."*

Craving is not just psychological, it is biological, and you can read a lot more about the science behind this in Chapter Two. What we crave, is largely determined by our socio-cultural environment. Alcohol, drugs and sex have long been an effective way of escaping pain and creating a feeling of euphoria. I would argue that sex is the most potent of these. God not only created us for His pleasure, but also for each other's. Sex is surely one of God's greatest gifts. What other experience offers us the same intensity of pleasure, euphoria and communion with another? Perhaps the exercise of our sexual drive is God's way of giving us a foretaste of the intimacies and ecstasies that await us in Heaven? Maybe that's why we crave sex so much?

Like so many addictive substances and behaviours, our craving for sexual intimacy and release can become an idol that gets in the way of our search for Him. The 'created' becomes more important than the 'Creator' and addiction becomes a counterfeit form of worship. We all worship the things that we love and esteem, indeed as Christians we believe we were created to worship. When our enthusiasm and joy overflows, we worship the source of that happiness, be that a partner, a child, a pastor, a piece of art, a football team, or any number of other things. But when we fail to put Christ first, or we assume our happiness should come from that source, we have become idol worshippers rather than true worshippers.

As I said earlier, in this preface, we are all addicts to a lesser or greater extent. And we are all worshippers. Kent Dunnington, in his helpful book 'Addiction and Virtue,' says:

> *"How is the saint really different from the addict who loses control over his life by submitting to the object of his addiction?"*

One key difference perhaps is the saint's *awareness* of idolatry as sin.

There is a morality about addiction – particularly sex addiction, which not just Christians, but society as a whole, uphold. Historically, addiction was viewed primarily as an issue relating to weak will and low moral values. An addict was someone who put their own selfish gain ahead of the needs of others. But the dynamics that continue addiction, namely: denial, deceit, fear, greed and selfishness are the same dynamics that are commonly found in almost every kind of sin. Whenever we sin we are putting our need for pleasure or solace ahead of our service of others and obedience to God.

If we are to consider addiction as a sin, we must ask ourselves if sin is the cause or the consequence? Many people with addiction have been victims of abuse, abandonment or rejection – and sadly, some of this has been at the hands of the Church or Christians. Addiction is perhaps not just the nature of humanity - God created us to crave His pleasures - but also a consequence of 'The Fall' as we seek comfort from the pleasures He provides outside of His will.

In addition to the spiritual perspective of understanding addiction, there are also biological, psychological and social aspects. Advances in neurobiological research have enabled us to see what happens in the brains of people with addiction and shown us that addictive behaviours change not only the reward system but also executive functioning. This explains not only the phenomenon of craving, withdrawal and escalation, but also why people continue to make decisions that will be harmful to themselves and others.

Research has also shown us that some people with addictions are genetically pre-disposed, either because of having a parent with an addiction or a concurrent mental health problem.

This has led to many people identifying addiction as a 'disease of the brain'. But others in the field of addiction focus on a psychological explanation, highlighting how addictive behaviours are used for emotional regulation and deeper underlying unresolved issues, often related to childhood insecurity and trauma. And then there are the social scientists who propose that it is our culture that encourages poor impulse control and provides easy access to a range of stimulants, rather than supporting growth in family life and community.

I hold what is known as a 'Biopsychosocial' approach to addiction which means that I believe that all three of these factors are true, and all need to be understood and addressed to overcome the problem.

Recovery or redemption?

Over the past 15 years that I've specialised in addiction I have met many esteemed colleagues who are themselves 'in recovery' from addiction. One thing that has fascinated me is how closely their recovery resembles the Christian conversion experience. They talk of being 'saved' from their addiction, of moving from a place of darkness to light, of feeling free from the chains of despair. Many who have been through a 12-step-process make reference to the steps, traditions and The Big Book, as Christians might make reference to the Bible. They talk of the support, challenge and encouragement of their community, as we might speak of the Church. And for most in recovery, they talk of developing new habits of surrender, meditation, gratitude and service, akin to common spiritual practices. The language of recovery and redemption are remarkably similar. As Christians, we believe that our redemption has already been secured, but we must claim it and walk in it. The same can be said of recovery. An alternative addiction-free lifestyle is always available, even though it may seem elusive and out of reach.

My journey as a psychotherapist has gone side-by-side with my spiritual journey as a Christian, and I have found that true healing only comes when body, mind and soul are in harmony. Some people might define soul as their deepest desires and instinctive sense of what's right and wrong. As Christians, we believe our soul belongs both with, and to, Christ. But whatever the definition, good mental health is found in those whose behaviours, thoughts and emotions are in accord with one another. When that happens, we enjoy a sense of integrity, authenticity and a meaningful and rewarding connection with others. Addiction shatters all of these things. In the grip of addiction our behaviours do not match what we feel in our hearts or know in our souls. We become disintegrated. And the secrecy and shame that accompanies addiction devastates honest, intimate connection with others.

Healing requires becoming whole again, and that demands changes in behaviours, feelings and our deepest desires. And as Christians, that means ensuring those desires are in line with God's will for our lives. Overcoming addiction is complex. In his book, "Not the

Way It's Supposed to Be", Cornelius Plantinga says:

> *"Like all sinners, the addict also needs painfully to unlearn old habits, to dismantle old scenarios, to pay old debts, and then to move steadfastly along the road to recovery one small, secure step at a time."*

It is my hope that this book might become a helpful guide on that journey.

CHAPTER ONE

Porn is in the
eye of the
beholder

What is pornography? Is it any naked image of the human form? Is it any image that's erotic? Is it always an image, or can words be pornographic too? When is something art? Erotica? Or porn? We will all have different ideas about what is pornographic, and what is not, and those views are largely influenced by the messages we've received about sex and sexuality from our childhood, our friends, our cultural environment and our church.

It's important to appreciate that there are many different viewpoints, and few of them are categorically wrong. Or rather, few are categorically wrong from a secular perspective. Hardly any would disagree that any kind of coercive or abusive sex is wrong and so are any images depicting it, but beyond that, the arguments often centre around taste, rather than morality. But as Christians, we are called to see the world through God's eyes, not our own.

Defining porn

Pornography is nothing new. Cave drawings showing exaggerated genitalia and fertility rituals have been found in various countries around the world dating from as early as 2,000 BC. It seems that mankind has always been fascinated by sex and sexuality, and, using the crudest of implements, have attempted to portray it. Human sexuality has also played a profound role in the belief systems of most of the world's cultures throughout the ages and in all major religions. When you consider that the gift of our sexuality allows us to perform the ultimate miracle and create life, there's little wonder that we both revere it, and fear it. It is also understandable that societies would strive to control such an intimate human act, which can have such significant social consequences.

Taboos around erotica have changed and evolved as societies have. The biggest ever haul of antique erotica came from Pompeii and was put on display until King Francis I of Naples ordered it to be removed. In the 15th century, the invention of the printing press allowed, not just printed erotic images, but also erotic stories to be widely distributed. After two hundred years of mixed reaction, obscenity laws were slowly introduced to protect the public from material that might 'deprave' or 'corrupt'. Obscenity laws continue today, but the definition of what is obscene, what is art, and what is simply 'freedom of human expression,' continues to be hotly debated.

As Christians, we are called to abide

by the laws of our land and our God. But the Bible says nothing explicitly about pornography, but rather about the sin of lust, which is often closely related. In Matthew 5:28 (ESV), Jesus says:

> *"But I say to you that everyone who looks at a woman with lustful intent has already committed adultery with her in his heart."*

Going beyond the traditional Jewish law of adultery as sin, Jesus says that lusting with the eyes is just as bad. So perhaps it is not so much the image itself that may be a sin, but the motivation of lust that's behind the viewing of it.

Some Christians might go further and say that viewing an image with lust is disrespectful, or even abusive. It reduces the physical form of one of God's creation to body parts to be objectified. Others might add that any portrayal of an intimate sexual encounter between a couple is wrong because this should remain private between the two. On the surface, this may seem to provide Christians with clear guidelines about what is sinful and what is not, but modern pornography provides loopholes. Loopholes that the addicted brain, when accompanied by technology, can easily get around.

There is now a whole genre of cartoon, animated and computer-generated porn that does not portray images of 'real' people. 'Hentai', 'anime' and 'manga' porn, all originally from Japan, are now some of the most popular types of porn viewed by young people. Another popular form of pornography on the internet is through the creation of avatars in a virtual world, where users can create images of their perfect partner, or partners, and interact with them sexually through an avatar of their ideal self. In addition, there is a growing amount of written pornography, some true life experiences expressed through the written word, whilst other writing is fictional or fantasy. Users can choose to read the stories of others, or write and publish their own.

It's often assumed that pornography is only attractive to men, but there is a growing number of women who find themselves addicted to porn; in fact an estimated 30% of sex addicts are female. There is now a growing industry of 'female-friendly' porn. A genre developed by feminist porn makers who were tired of the way that women were portrayed as sexual objects, and chose to turn the tables and provide material more arousing to the modern woman. In addition to visual material, the web is now heavily populated with erotic stories, written by women, for women – a market that exploded in the wake of the highly popular "Fifty Shades of Grey" book trilogy.

Recent technological advances and the internet have provided countless different ways of being sexual, both alone and with others, in anonymous, accessible and affordable ways. Regrettably, many people, especially those in the grip of addiction, escalate to sexual talk with others in chat rooms, browsing adult profiles on sex worker sites and 'hook up' sites, watching live sexual acts via webcam or sharing their own sexual acts virtually. Others escalate further to visiting sex workers or meeting strangers for casual sex. Whatever your age, gender, race, faith, orientation, physical or mental ability, geography, financial means or pretty much anything else, it's easier to find and enjoy sex now than it has been at any other time in history. And since the advent of the smart phone, access to sexual stimuli can literally be available, anytime and anywhere.

As the opportunities and temptations for pornography increase, so the boundaries blur between what is real and what is not. The debate of what God may or may not approve of needs some foundations, so it is helpful to consider what His true intention was for creating us as sexual beings.

God's gift of sexuality

The bottom line is that God did not have to give us sexuality, nor genitals through which to experience our sex drive. If He had wanted to, we could have been single sex creatures and reproduced in an alternative way. And He certainly didn't have to give the pleasure of sexual and sensual sensation to both men and women. It's still not known if other animals experience orgasm in the same way as humans do, particularly females, but it is known that many other species mate for pleasure, not just for reproduction. If you think about it, that's obvious – most mammals would not have the cognitive capacity to make the decision to start a family – they have sex because it's pleasurable.

But it is much more than just pleasurable, it is bonding. Scientists have known for some time that when couples touch they produce a chemical called 'oxytocin,' which increases feelings of closeness and intimacy. And when we orgasm, we get a sudden surge of this chemical which bonds us even closer still. So when God said, "Go forth and multiply," (see Genesis 9:7) He knew that it would not be a task, but a pleasure, and a pleasure that would bond His people together.

Another of God's gifts to us is erotic empathy. Have you ever wondered why we are the only species on the planet that has sex in private? You might think it's due to societal pressures for modesty, but if that were the case it would not be so prevalent across almost all cultures throughout history. Evolutionary psychologists suggest that it's about protection and safety, as we are at our most vulnerable when having sex. But that's true for all creatures, so why don't they bother?

The gift of erotic empathy means that we are the only species that gets aroused when we see our partner get aroused. A bored or uninterested lover is a turn off, whereas an enthusiastic, uninhibited lover who confidently displays their sexual enjoyment is a massive turn on. The evolutionary psychologists may be right that we are more vulnerable, because if we were to have sex in public, others would want to watch, or even join in! Erotic empathy is a wonderful gift that allows couples to be enthralled by each other's passion, but this is also the reason why people watch pornography. In short, seeing others turned on, turns us on. But regrettably for some, when we get turned on – it seems impossible to find the 'off' button.

Someone once quipped that when God created the human sex drive, He gave us the engine of a Ferrari and the brakes of a bicycle! How true that is for the many who struggle with sex and porn addiction. But it's no joking matter. The strength of drive does, of course, vary from person to person, and we know that male sex drive, which is governed by testosterone, is generally stronger than women's. Struggling with the power of our sex drive is nothing new. The early Church fathers also struggled. St Augustine famously prayed,

> *"Give me chastity.... but not yet."*

While St Jerome complained whilst fasting in the desert,

> *"I fancied myself among bevies of girls... my mind was burning with the cravings of desire, and the fires of lust flared up from my flesh that was as that of a corpse".*

These fearful desires led to sex being deemed an obstacle to holiness and a sin, and a whole variety of laws were put in place to limit it. These rules were backed up with weak theological arguments that reinforced the practices of asceticism and celibacy. But those rules miss the point. It isn't sex that is the sin, nor the drive for it, but rather the potential consequences that occur when it's used outside of God's guidelines.

How culture distorts God's gift of sex

When God gave us sex, He also gave us guidelines for how to use it. It didn't come with a guarantee that it would be fantastic every time, nor that we could do it whenever, wherever and with whoever we wanted. Whilst arguments continue over whether sex should be confined to the modern definition of marriage, as opposed to early biblical examples of betrothal and polygamy, it's clear that sex was designed for committed relationships. And within that context, we are free to enjoy God's gift.

Modern society has simultaneously under-rated and over-sold sex. And many churches and Christian teachings are also guilty of this. The bottom line is that sex has the 'potential' to be an amazing experience between loving couples, but that is not always the case. No matter how much you love someone, sex can be awkward, embarrassing, disappointing, boring, painful and unrewarding. And if you've experienced any kind of abuse in the past, or received negative sexual messages, it can be frightening. The media tells us that sex is fantastic, and great sex can be had by anyone, or rather, by almost anyone. The people we see on our screens or read about in magazines are predominantly young, beautiful, fit and healthy – and it seems that great sex makes them happy. Christians can inadvertently fuel this myth by focusing what limited teaching they provide on sex and sexuality to young people and implying that the reward of a happy sex life will automatically come with marriage.

The prevalence of porn and our sexualised culture obviously doesn't help. We are bombarded with images of beauty and automatically associate sexuality with sexual activity. But where does that leave those who choose to be celibate or chaste? Furthermore, society tells us that our worth is based on our sexual attractiveness. Positive images of masculinity are embellished with illusions of sexual conquest, while positive feminine images exude sexual desirability. And when you combine these messages, many find themselves left with a conundrum – I must be sexy, but not a 'slut' or a 'lad'. These overt and covert messages about sexuality have a significant impact on people today and like much of our sexual culture, they are a million miles from what God intended.

It is these views that force us to either over-sexualise ourselves and try to compete with our pornified culture, or deny and repress our sexual needs out of fear of moral judgment. For some, the split is extreme, "Would I prefer my spouse to view me as a porn star, or a prude?"

The truth is, we should all be seen as God created us, as – "fearfully and wonderfully made" (Psalm 139:14 NIV).

"God created man in His own

image...male and female he created them" (Genesis 1:27 NIV). Shame about our naked physical bodies was not part of God's plan - it was a result of the fall. Genesis 2:25 (ESV) says, "and the man and his wife were both naked and were not ashamed".

But contrary to popular belief, not all pornography is of beautiful people, and that's why some are drawn to it. In 'pornland' you can find any kind of body type you like, which for some is a comfort as it demonstrates that sex is not confined to the fit and fabulous few. And many people turn to the internet for advice and sex education, some of which can be graphic and some that might be considered porn. Information, guidance and reassurance are sometimes the reasons why people look at porn, at least initially, rather than lust. And with an absence of positive sexual information, we must acknowledge that we are, at least in part, to blame.

God's plan for sex is a great one, but the teaching we read in the Bible is limited to the days in which it was written. As Christians, we have a responsibility to help people through the modern maze of negative influences and messages. We see similar challenges in learning how to manage other aspects of our lives, such as our finances, our ambitions and our diet. Seeking God's plan for us within our cultural context, and separating it from other influences, is often not easy.

Evaluating your sexual influences

How you feel about yourself as a sexual human being and how you believe sex should, and could be, starts in early childhood and continues to change and grow, as we get older.

In early childhood, those messages come from our parents. From the first moment you inquisitively put your hand down your pants, or decided to take them off altogether, you would have learnt something from your parent's response. Our parents are hugely influential in what they say, and in what they don't say. We learn whether or not nudity and sex is natural, private, rude or wrong - long before we know what it is.

As your body began to change during puberty, parental messages were joined by the voices of your peers. If your family celebrated your changing body then you're more likely to be confident about your sexuality now, but if you were made to feel embarrassed you may have become self-conscious. If you developed at the same time as your peers the physical changes will have felt like a normal part of growing up. But if you were a particularly late or early developer you may have developed feelings of doubt and anxiety.

Our early sexual experiences are also key influences. Some are introduced to sex, long before the emotional and cognitive centres of the brain can make sense of it. Either through abuse, or by stumbling across porn, or being introduced to it by older peers. If you were brought up in a Christian household, you may have had little sexual experience, or you may have 'experimented' as many adolescents do. Those times of experimentation may have been safe and enjoyable, but they may have left you with fears, doubts or unrealistic expectations for future sexual encounters. Or if you had little or no sexual experimentation, you may feel that you missed out – especially if sex in later life has not turned out to be as you assumed it would. Many young Christians who have 'saved themselves for marriage', complain of bitter disappointment and feel cheated out of opportunities that their contemporaries may have enjoyed. Conversely, some Christians who were sexually active before marriage, feel such shame and remorse, that they unconsciously sabotage their chance of sexual fulfillment within their relationships.

WHAT FOLLOWS IS AN EXERCISE THAT CAN HELP YOU TO CONSIDER WHAT MESSAGES YOU'VE PICKED UP ABOUT SEX OVER THE YEARS. LOOK AT THE LIST OF WORDS AND CHOOSE AS MANY AS YOU LIKE TO DESCRIBE THE FOLLOWING...

HOW YOU FELT ABOUT SEX WHEN YOU WERE GROWING UP?

HOW YOU FEEL ABOUT SEX NOW?

NOW LOOK OVER THE LIST OF WORDS YOU'VE HIGHLIGHTED AND CONSIDER HOW THIS COMPARES WITH GOD'S VIEW OF SEX AND HOW HE WANTS YOU TO FEEL ABOUT YOUR SEXUALITY.

Exercise

EXCITING EROTIC
INTENSE GENTLE DUTIFUL
ENERGETIC THRILLING
ECSTATIC PASSIONATE
SORDID URGENT PRIMITIVE
DISGUSTING RUDE LOVING
EMBARRASSING IMMATURE
PAINFUL BORING BONDING
UNHOLY THREATENING
FRIGHTENING REASSURING
HAPPY SATISFYING COSY
INTIMATE ROMANTIC
FUN MYSTICAL RELAXING
SENSUAL SHAMEFUL WARM
UNIFYING MEMORABLE
EMOTIONAL MAGICAL
SILLY DANGEROUS DIRTY
POINTLESS ROUTINE SAD
UPLIFTING GENEROUS
UNCOMFORTABLE
DEPRESSING TIRING

Deciding what's right for you?

Whatever your history, your gender, your age, physical ability and relationshal status, God intended you to enjoy your sexuality and express it in line with His will. If completing the exercise has left you recognising that some of your feelings about sex are not as He intended, then you may benefit from talking to someone about this or reading further on positive Christian sexuality. (There are some book suggestions for you in Chapter Seven). If you have had particularly painful or abusive sexual experiences in your past, then you might also find it helpful to work through these issues with a professional counsellor.

If you're in the grip of sex or porn addiction, then you already know that this is not what God intended for you. We will go on to explore how you can break free of your addiction in later chapters. But first, I'd like to invite you to think about how you want to feel about your sexuality and what healthy sexuality, as a Christian, means for you.

Go back to the list of words again, but this time highlight the ones that express how you want to feel about your sex life. You could write them here:

As we have seen, it is not easy to discern God's will for your sex life. Indeed, it is often difficult to work out what God wants from us in many areas of our lives.

We can be faced with lots of questions can't we? There are significant challenges to Christians today as the sexual attitudes around us continue to become increasingly permissive and inclusive.

If you're hoping to find an answer in these pages of what is right for you, in your particular sexual situation and circumstances, then I'm sorry, but you may not find it.

For example, you may be thinking things like:

Is it ok to masturbate if I only imagine my partner?

Is it ok to masturbate if I focus only on the sensual physical sensation, rather than any external stimuli?

Is it ok to read erotic literature to create the mood for partnered sex?

Is it ok to view only animated porn?

Is it ok to watch a sex educational video to improve my technique?

And if so, must I turn it off if I find I am feeling aroused?

Or there may be a myriad of other things on your mind. I can't offer any answers to these kinds of personal questions, I'm afraid. Those are things you must bring to God and ask for His revelation about.

What I do hope is that you will learn more in this book about what God's best looks like for you in this area and be encouraged on your journey to express your sexuality in line with His heart.

PAULA HALL

Reflection

In this chapter we have explored:

- God's view versus culture's view of sex and sexuality
- How our attitudes to sexuality are formed
- Discerning how God wants you to feel about sex

Before moving on to the next chapter, take some time now to reflect on the passages below.

"All things are lawful for me – but not everything is beneficial. All things are lawful for me – but I will not be controlled by anything. Food is for the stomach and the stomach is for food, but God will do away with both. The body is not for sexual immorality, but for the Lord, and the Lord for the body."

(1 CORINTHIANS 6:12-13 NET)

"For this is God's will: that you become holy, that you keep away from sexual immorality, that each of you know how to possess his own body in holiness and honor, not in lustful passion like the Gentiles who do not know God."

(1 THESSALONIANS 4:3-5 NET)

WHICH WORDS OR PHRASES RESONATE WITH YOU AT THE MOMENT?

WHY DO YOU THINK THAT IS?

CONSIDER WHAT CHANGES GOD MAY BE CALLING YOU TO MAKE IN YOUR SEXUAL ATTITUDES AND BEHAVIOUR.

YOU MAY WANT TO MAKE A NOTE OF WHAT YOU FEEL HE IS DRAWING YOUR ATTENTION TO.

WHAT CAN YOU PRAY AS A RESULT OF THIS REFLECTION?

IS THERE ANYTHING PRACTICAL YOU COULD START OR STOP DOING?

Reflection Notes

> "Fall down seven times, stand up eight."
>
> – JAPANESE PROVERB

CHAPTER TWO

Porn on the brain

The problem with writing anything scientific, especially connected to neuroscience, is that it could be out of date by the time the book is in print, let alone a year or two later! But, in this chapter I'm going to share with you the latest research and current thinking on how addiction affects the brain – and in particular, why porn can be particularly addictive. But please do be aware that there will undoubtedly be more recent studies and reports in addition to what's written here. Also, I am not a neuroscientist, nor an academic, so you won't find a whole load of jargon here. The aim of this chapter is to help you understand how addiction happens and why it's so hard to stop.

Furthermore, although this chapter aims to explain what happens in the brain, I want to highlight that God created us to be so much more than a few billion neurons. We are body, mind and soul, and as you will see in subsequent chapters, addiction affects every part of our human experience.

The neuroscience of addiction

Addiction has been studied for many years and it is now widely understood that addictive behaviours, as well as substances, change the architecture of the brain. What starts as a habit, becomes increasingly entrenched over time until the behaviour becomes almost automatic. These brain changes are often referred to as 'conditioning'. A common phrase in the field of neuroscience is 'neurons that fire together, wire together'. In other words, the more often you repeat a behaviour, the stronger the neural connection in your brain becomes. In many respects, addiction is simply a 'learnt' behaviour. Whenever we learn something, our brain changes and the more we practise, the more automatic what we've learnt becomes. For example, when we first learn to drive a car or use a new piece of computer software it is difficult, or may even seem impossible. But, if we keep practising, it will become automatic. The fancy word for this is 'neurogenesis'. Our brains are highly malleable; whatever we learn and however we learn it, we create new neural connections in our brain. And the more we practice it, the stronger the neural pathways become and the more automatic a behaviour becomes. So, in the simplest of terms, we learn to become addicted, and regrettably, unlearning is often harder than learning.

We now know that some brains are more susceptible to learning addiction than others. Research has shown that those with a genetic history of addiction, in other words, those who have family members who have, or had, an addiction, are more likely to become addicted themselves. Furthermore, recent research has shown that the developing adolescent brain is particularly vulnerable to addiction. Adolescence is a time when our brains are highly impressionable, which means not only is it easier to 'teach a young dog new tricks,' but it's also easier to get it hooked on unhealthy behaviours and substances.

One of the reasons why addiction can become so firmly rooted is because it encompasses the three major parts of our brain. Our survival brain, our emotional brain and our thinking brain. We'll look at each of these in turn.

THE SURVIVAL BRAIN

The first part of our brain to come 'online' when we're born is our survival brain, sometimes referred to as the 'reptilian brain', and its sole responsibility is to help us survive. All species have a 'reptilian brain' – even reptiles (hence the name.) It's the part of us that makes us jump when we watch a scary movie, or flinch when we touch something hot. We have no conscious control over it – its primary function is simply to keep us alive in times of danger. It provides us with the instinctive responses of fight, flight or freeze, long before we have time to think or emotionally feel anything.

Our survival brain acts like an alarm bell, warning us that we are in danger and we need to do something fast. The problem is, that like all alarm bells, sometimes they get triggered when there is no actual threat. People who have experienced trauma, whether that's as a child or in adulthood, can find themselves with a survival brain that keeps going off when it shouldn't. Addiction often becomes a way of coping with these false alarms. So the addictive behaviour becomes a way of surviving. You can read more on this in Chapter 3.

THE EMOTIONAL BRAIN

The second part of the brain to come online is the emotional brain, also known as our 'limbic system.' The emotional brain is the part that's responsible for emotion, behaviour, memory and motivation. It's where we store our memories and feel our emotions. And where we develop basic behavioural skills that are important to us as a species. For example, this system moderates behaviours such as sleeping and eating, as well as motivating us for social bonding activities such as caring, playing and having sex.

The emotional brain is also where our reward centre resides. We know that the more reward we experience, the greater the desire there will be to seek it out and the deeper it will be imprinted onto our memory. The memory is stored deeper still if we experienced a reward greater than anticipated. That's why we never forget that amazing meal at the run down café that we'd turned our noses up at, or the amazing worship experience at a church we didn't really want to go to. It's also why we continue to go back to see if we can relive the experience or keep seeking the experience in other places. This link between reward and memory also explains why a particularly powerful sexual image or encounter can become entrenched in our mind.

THE THINKING BRAIN

The last part of our brain to develop is the 'neocortex', aka the thinking brain. Our thinking brain is responsible for rational processing of information and decision-making. It's the home of logic and reason and the bit of us that separates us from the rest of God's creation. Our thinking brain gives us the tools to understand what's happening in our survival and emotional brain and decide how to respond. But unfortunately, sometimes those decisions are wrong and/or they happen too slowly.

God designed us to put our survival, and the survival of our species, first. That's why we often make stupid mistakes when we feel threatened, but it is also why we're capable of heroic acts of bravery to save others. We instinctively notice danger, then feel our emotional and physical response, then decide what to do, based on that initial instinct. That makes absolute sense when the danger is real, but when it's a false alarm, it may lead us to behave irrationally. Addictions are often irrational responses to perceived threats that have become entrenched in our brain through repetition.

Before we move on from neuroscience, there's another key element that's worth knowing about. Or rather, a chemical, not an element – and that's dopamine.

DOPAMINE

Dopamine is the common denominator in all addictions. It is the neurotransmitter that sends the messages between the neurons that create the neural pathways to make those connections stronger and stronger. Dopamine is the chemical that is responsible for motivation. It makes us 'want' to do things that are pleasurable and 'drives' us to seek them out. But, contrary to popular belief, it is not, in itself, responsible for creating the sensation of pleasure. Dopamine makes us crave, but it is other chemicals such as serotonin, endorphin and opioids that make us enjoy and feel satisfied. That's why so many people with addiction 'want' to do things that they don't like and don't feel satisfied afterwards.

If you're not someone with an addiction and you're struggling to make sense of that, remember the last time you got the munchies for something sweet? It's late at night and you're hunting the fridge and the cupboards, preferably for a forgotten chunk of chocolate. But all you can find is a stale biscuit at the bottom of the barrel. In your heart of hearts, you know this is not going to do the job, but you eat it anyway. If dopamine keeps up its job, you won't give up and might find yourself putting on your coat and heading out to the local garage or corner shop, in spite of the howling wind and rain! When dopamine 'wants' something, common sense often goes out of the window.

We also know that dopamine production surges with novelty. The 'same old, same old' gets boring over time – no matter what it is. We all enjoy something that is new and exciting, whether it's the latest mobile technology, a new car or the latest Bond film. Perhaps God gave us this gift to encourage us to keep learning and to continue to crave new experiences with Him?

Dopamine is also responsible for what's known as escalation. Escalation is the term used to describe how addictive behaviours either take up more and more time, or become more extreme. Dopamine is a tricky chemical to satisfy – because the more we get - the more we want. This is often referred to as tolerance. This is because as cravings intensify, more dopamine is produced from the 'sending neuron' and after a while, the 'receiving neuron' gets flooded and begins to close down some of its receptors. This results in the sending neuron pumping out even more. If you imagine dopamine as sound, the sending neuron is the volume and the receptor is your ears. As you turn the volume up, you will cover your ears to protect yourself from the volume. But the radio wants to be heard and so it will turn the volume up even louder, forcing you to cover your ears even more firmly – and so the cycle continues. The original volume level can no longer be heard and so it must continue to escalate. This is true of addictive behaviours and hence people with porn addiction will often find themselves spending longer and longer periods of time or viewing more and more explicit material, in order to get the same dopamine effect.

Before we leave dopamine and escalation behind, there is one other thing that you need to know about it. The more you produce, the less motivation you have for other activities and the less enjoyment you get from them. Back to the radio metaphor – as the volume goes up and up on your radio you become increasingly deaf to other sounds. That's why people with addiction often become less and less interested in other areas of their lives. Motivation for relationships, friendships, hobbies, learning, travel – and of course spirituality are all gradually eroded, as addiction takes an ever stronger grip on our desires.

Why porn is so powerful

Whether you're an evolutionist, a creationist, or a bit of both, it's impossible to deny that we were created to enjoy the physical form of others and that we like a bit of variety every now and again. To keep our appetite going, whether that's for food or sex, we generally need the menu to change. No matter how much you love rice pudding, you wouldn't want it for every meal! Most couples in long-term relationships would testify that changing their sexual routines and techniques is a helpful way to keep the home fires burning. Curiosity may have killed the cat, but familiarity can kill even the most ardent sex kitten. Evolutionary theory would say that this is all about our innate need to spread the gene pool and we are instinctively drawn to body parts that suggest fertility. Hence big breasts are unlikely to go out of fashion and neither are a muscular pair of pecs. Whatever the reason for this, human experience tells us it's true.

We are all drawn to stimuli that are programmed into us for survival, be that nutritious food sources or fertile humans. But when those stimuli are exaggerated, they are known as 'supernormal stimuli'. The donut is a good example of this. Researchers have found that the humble ring donut is the perfect balance of fat, carbs and sugar that our limbic system craves and most of us get a flood of dopamine when we see one. Hopefully our neocortex kicks in to stop us eating a dozen of them at once, but the desire is normal and commonplace. Pornography is another form of supernormal stimuli. Whilst we seek an occasional bit of variety and our head may be turned by an attractive body part, pornography provides us with endless novelty and exaggerated images of fertility. But unlike donuts, the physical consequences are often much harder to spot and hence we can binge on porn without knowing the impact that it is having on us.

Not only is porn a supernormal stimulus, but it is also easily and freely accessible. Most of us wouldn't binge on donuts 24/7, even if there were no obvious side effects to our health and we lived in a world with no vanity. We wouldn't do it, simply because we would get bored of them. But pornography provides endless novelty that keeps the craving going and the dopamine pumping out. internet pornography has been called the crack-cocaine of sex addiction and people in the field of internet addiction say that pornography is the most addictive substance available online. Internet porn is free, easily accessible, highly addictive and appears to have no harmful consequences – until it's too late.

Sexual dysfunctions and other side effects

The side effects of heavy porn use often aren't noticed until the brain has already rewired itself to porn as the optimum source of sexual reward. Below is a list of the most common consequences of porn use. These also double up as being the most common symptoms that pornography use is a problem. Please note, this list is primarily linked to what is happening in the brain, and is in no particular order. The impact on couple relationships is explored later in the book.

DIFFICULTY REACHING ORGASM

This may be the first sign that porn use is becoming a problem. If you're in a relationship, then you may notice that it takes longer and longer to experience orgasm and you may find yourself having to resort to fantasy, or remembering porn images, in order to climax at all. This is because your brain and body has got so used to high level stimulation that it now needs it, in order to perform. Assuming of course, you manage to get turned on in the first place.

ERECTILE DYSFUNCTION

Similar to above, as your brain and body gradually become conditioned to high level stimuli for arousal, over time you will find it difficult to become aroused at all without those stimuli. For men of course, this is going to be most noticeable by the fact that you can't get an erection, but the process is the same for women too. Rates of erection problems in young men are increasing as more and more are reporting what is becoming known as Porn Induced Erectile Dysfunction – PIED for short. The good news is that this is reversible over time.

DEPRESSION, LETHARGY AND PROCRASTINATION

Earlier in this chapter we were seeing how dopamine

is the chemical responsible for motivation and if it all becomes directed in one place, desire for other activities can diminish. The overall effect of this is often a general feeling of lethargy. Many porn addicts find it increasingly difficult to summon the motivation to do anything and even the simplest of tasks can be continually postponed. Work or study deadlines suffer and the 'to do' list gets longer and longer. Over time, life can feel overwhelmingly hard and a real sense of depression may descend. Unfortunately, porn may feel like the cure to these painful feelings, but in reality it is often the cause. Giving up porn provides the opportunity to discover if there are underlying issues that need to be addressed that the porn was masking.

SOCIAL ANXIETY

Over recent years a number of people have written about the links between social anxiety and heavy porn use. The most obvious cause for this is simply that if you spend most of your time in front of a screen, as opposed to mixing with other people, then your social skills will suffer and you're likely to become more anxious. But other theories suggest it is dopamine that is responsible. As we were seeing earlier, dopamine is the chemical responsible for motivation for every activity in life and chronic porn use reduces the amount of dopamine available for those activities. Social situations and relationships simply aren't as appealing to dopamine as pornography and as you withdraw from social interactions, anxieties can rise. Many people, including some professionals, mistakenly think that social anxiety is the cause of addiction, but in reality, it is often the consequence.

OBJECTIFICATION

Most heavy porn users become aware that they struggle to look at people without sexualising them – especially attractive people. Rather than seeing the full human being, the person created by God in His image, they see body parts that entice and excite. Even with exerted effort, it becomes difficult to focus on conversations with others, without the mind, and sometimes the eyes, wandering. This struggle is not purely psychological, it is physiological. Researchers have shown that people with addiction adopt what is known as an 'attentional bias' towards visual cues relating to their addiction. For example, a smoker who has recently given up can pick up a whiff of cigarette smoke long before a non-smoker. And an alcoholic will notice an empty bottle of wine upturned in a bin where anyone else may have overlooked it. Most people find that this tendency naturally diminishes when they've stopped viewing porn for a period of time, but there's further advice on how to stop this in Chapter Five.

DIVERSE SEXUAL TASTES

Many people with porn addiction worry about their sexual tastes, and sometimes also, their sexual orientation. The internet pornworld caters for every sexual taste imaginable and as we were seeing earlier, dopamine thrives on novelty. This means that as tolerance develops, many people find themselves looking at more extreme images in order to get the same level of arousal. This can create huge levels of anxiety as people find themselves attracted to sexual images and practices that ordinarily, they would find disturbing. Remember – dopamine is all about wanting, not necessarily about liking something.

Another explanation for this is that high levels of dopamine are thought to temporarily switch off our innate disgust response. So during a heavy dopamine-fuelled porn session, a whole variety of images may be used to maintain arousal, but as soon as it's over, the disgust response kicks in leaving the user feeling confused and ashamed.

The other component at play here is sexual conditioning. As we saw earlier, addictions are learnt behaviours, so the more often you view a particular type of image or genre of porn, the stronger the connections in your brain become. And the more novel it is, the better – as far as dopamine is concerned. This leaves some porn users assuming that a certain genre must be their 'natural' taste or orientation, but in reality, it's a trick of the brain – one that may be reversed when porn use ends.

OFFENDING

Dopamine's endless quest for novelty leads some porn users into viewing illegal sexual images such as bestiality and underage porn. And sadly, this is not unusual. In the survey I undertook for my other book - 'Understanding & Treating Sex Addiction,' 31% of people had viewed bestiality images, 9% had viewed a child image and 50% had viewed teenage porn. It's important to know that 'underage' means any image of a person under the age of 18. Although it is legal in our country to have sex at 16, it is illegal to view any sexualised image of someone under the age of 18.

The viewing of underage images is a growing problem within our society and one that many people are working hard to overcome. It's widely accepted that the easy availability of internet pornography is to blame, and contrary to popular belief, it is very easy to find underage porn – often accidentally. For some, this is the rock bottom moment that finally makes them realise how out of control their porn use has become and begin to seek help.

There is a common assumption that anyone who has viewed an underage image is a risk to children and young people. This misconception can be hugely damaging as it adds shame on top of shame and can have devastating consequences on someone's life if they are reported to the authorities. When viewing an underage image is an escalation of addiction, overcoming the addiction is the primary need. Any risk assessment concerns should be left to professionals working in this field who would make the necessary referral to authorities if required. If you, or someone you know, is viewing disturbing images and you are unsure what to do, turn to Chapter 7 where you will find a list of organisations to advise you.

Remember – dopamine is about wanting, not liking; it thrives on novelty and temporarily switches off the disgust response. Unfortunately, dopamine, residing in our emotional brain, does not discriminate between right and wrong. But as the thinking brain comes back online after viewing, the remorse, regret and shame can be overwhelming.

Retraining your brain

Most of the information on overcoming addiction is in Chapter Five, but since we're talking about the brain, this seems like a good place to introduce the concepts of 'rebooting' and 'rewiring'.

REBOOTING

Rebooting is a term that is now widely used by people giving up porn, to describe the process of stopping their porn use in order to restore their brain to its original factory settings. It is known that we can't completely unlearn, but our brains can become increasingly forgetful. The neural pathways never completely disappear, but over time, they will become weaker and weaker.

Giving up porn allows the brain the opportunity to restore its sensitivity to other, everyday pleasures. It will also reduce the intensity of cravings and give the thinking brain a chance to get its common sense back.

REWIRING

The process of rewiring means establishing new neural pathways to sources of dopamine that give genuine pleasure and satisfaction in life. In other words, it's about re-learning. Like rebooting, this also takes time. New habits and activities, developed over time, will become increasingly hardwired and automatic.

Sex and pornography addiction affect the wiring of the brain. Understanding this is critical to breaking through the shame that so often continues it. Addiction is crazy and for some, makes little logical sense.

Why do we keep on doing something that we don't want to do and frequently get very little pleasure from?

Why do we break our own value systems and do what we know is wrong?

Why do we look at pornography that disgusts us?

Why do we risk our marriages and our relationship with God for something that has no meaning to us?

The answer to these questions is, because God gave us an amazing brain and a wonderful chemical called dopamine that motivates us to seek ever more of His glory and pleasure. As with so many things in our fallen world, the devil has taken what God meant for good and turned it into something else. But by God's grace, you can take it back. Keep reading…

PAULA HALL

Reflection

In this chapter we have explored:

- Why pornography is so powerful
- How pornography changes the architecture of the brain
- The side effects of compulsive pornography use
- The basic principles of rewiring your brain

"I praise you because I am fearfully and wonderfully made, your works are wonderful, I know that full well."
(PSALM 139:14 NIV)

WHAT DOES THIS VERSE MEAN TO YOU AT THE MOMENT?

IS THERE A CHALLENGE IN THOSE WORDS FOR YOU?

YOU MAY LIKE TO WRITE YOUR REFLECTIONS DOWN.

The human body is truly amazing. Billions and billions of cells created by God to make each of us unique, but all in the image of Him. The verse above is a celebration of God's incredible design of the human body, but there's also a challenge in here too. Most theologians interpret 'fearfully' to mean 'with reverence and respect'. In other words, we are called to revere and respect God's creation of us, but perhaps also, revere and respect our body because it was created by God. We may never fully understand the complexities of the human brain, but God does and He created it for His purpose.

REFLECT ON THE FOLLOWING:

HOW DOES IT FEEL TO KNOW THAT GOD CREATED A BRAIN THAT CAN BECOME ADDICTED?

WHAT DO YOU THINK GOD WANTS YOU TO BE 'ADDICTED' TO?

WHAT DIFFERENCE WOULD IT MAKE IN YOUR LIFE IF YOU WERE TO HAVE REVERENCE TOWARDS AND RESPECT THE DESIGN OF YOUR BRAIN?

Reflection Notes

> "If you hear a voice within you say 'you cannot paint', then by all means paint and that voice will be silenced."

— VINCENT VAN GOGH

CHAPTER THREE

Facing the truth

How do you know if your pornography viewing is a problem? Well the short answer is that if you're seeking sexual gratification through porn and you're a Christian – it is a problem. No matter how often you do it and whether you want to stop or not, there are no Biblical or theological arguments that support the use of pornography for a Christian man or woman. Is it a sin greater than any other? Probably not, but like all sins, it has consequences – whether your use is compulsive or not.

This chapter will help you to think about your pornography use and the impact it has on you, on those around you and on your relationship with God. You'll also find questions to help you consider if your viewing is compulsive and whether or not it has developed into an addiction that you need help to overcome. We'll start by looking at the consequences of watching porn, but first let's talk about denial.

Breaking denial

Denial is common amongst not only addicts, but sinners too. Denial is a supremely effective form of self deception that refuses to acknowledge that we are doing something wrong, even though we know deep down that we are. Our Christian conscience tells us what we should do and our hunger for integrity and wholeness makes us want to behave within our conscience. Romans 7 talks of this inward battle between knowing what's right and doing what's right. In verse 15 Paul says, "I don't really understand myself, for I want to do what is right, but I don't do it. Instead I do what I hate" (NLT). Denial is a defense mechanism against shame, a strategy that allows us to live with a false sense of integrity.

Denial works in a number of cunning ways. If you're reading this book, then it's unlikely that you're in total denial, but you may be struggling to fully acknowledge and accept the extent of your problem. You may be minimising it and telling yourself 'it's not as bad as...', or 'I know it's a sin but I'll stop when...'; or you may be justifying and saying 'I can't stop because...'; or perhaps blaming others and denying full responsibility. All of these are ways of denying the truth that you should and can stop.

For the Christian, the antidote to denial is grace and faith. Grace tells us that nothing can separate us from the love of God - "For I am convinced that neither death nor life, neither angels nor demons, neither the present nor the future, nor any powers, neither height nor depth, nor anything else in all creation, will be able to separate us from the love of God that is in Christ Jesus our Lord" (Romans 8:38-39 NIV). Grace promises us that when we acknowledge and confess our sins, we will be brought to wholeness.

> *"If we claim to be without sin, we deceive ourselves and the truth is not in us. If we confess our sins, he is faithful and just and will forgive us our sins and purify us from all unrighteousness. If we claim we have not sinned, we make him out to be a liar and his word is not in us."*
> **(1 JOHN 1: 8-10 NIV)**

> *"Faith assures us that God is in control and He knows our needs and can and will provide for them. When we walk in that faith, we can become free to see our lives through His eyes. Jesus said, "If you hold to my teaching, you are really my disciples. Then you will know the truth, and the truth will set you free."*
> **(JOHN 8: 31,32 NIV)**

With truth comes conviction. Jesus said that when the Holy Spirit came, he would convict us of our sins (See John 16:8). Now that might sound fearful but if you understand grace and faith, then conviction is something we should seek, so that we can begin to live the life God promises. Before you move forward in this chapter, consider praying or meditating on one of the Psalms below.

> *"Search me, God, and know my heart; test me and know my anxious thoughts. See if there is any offensive way in me, and lead me in the way everlasting."*
> **PSALM 139: 23-24 (NIV)**

> *"Who can see his own mistakes?*
> *Forgive my sins that I do not see*
> *And keep Your servant from sinning by*
> *going my own way.*
> *Do not let these sins rule over me.*
> *Then I will be without blame.*
> *And I will not be found guilty of big sins."*
> **PSALM 19:12-13 (NLT)**

The consequence of porn

What impact is viewing pornography having on your life? Take a look at the list below and tick the boxes that best describe your situation. If you want to be sure you're not in denial of the extent of the actual or potential consequences of your porn use, then you could share this exercise with a trusted friend, pastoral advisor, spiritual director or counsellor who can help you examine each question in depth.

THE CONSEQUENCES OF PORN	YES	NO	MAYBE
It gets in the way of developing relationships			
It affects intimacy between my spouse and I			
It damages how I feel about myself			
I spend less time with friends and family			
It affects how close I feel to God			
I spend less time on health, fitness, hobbies, personal and spiritual growth			
It gets in the way of my work			
It compromises my work and career			
It has led me to other sexual behaviours that contravene my value system			
It tempts me to engage in other sexual behaviours that contravene my value system			
It affects how I view people around me			
It negatively influences my sexual expectations			
If others knew of my porn use, I would feel very ashamed			
If others knew of my porn use, I would risk losing something valuable to me			

Pornography use, whether it's addictive or not, affects every area of someone's life. It's tempting to think that as long as no one knows, there are no consequences, but that is an illusion. Secrecy always comes at a cost. It costs our sense of personal integrity and how close we can get to others and God. If you answered 'yes' or 'maybe' to most of the questions, then your problem is more likely to be compulsive, but the following questions will help to confirm that. As before, if you fear you may struggle to be fully honest with yourself, find someone you can trust who will both challenge and support you.

Am I addicted?

1. Do you feel as though your behaviour has a significant negative impact on the life you lead or the life you want?

2. Have you tried to stop, or limit your pornography viewing in the past and repeatedly failed?

3. Has your pornography use increased in amount of time, or in more extreme genres of porn?

4. Has your pornography use escalated to other online or offline sexual activities?

5. Are you more likely to watch porn when you're struggling with difficult emotions such as anxiety, stress, irritability, loneliness, sadness or depression?

6. Do you feel dependent on porn, or fantasise about porn, for sexual release?

7. Are you pre-occupied by thoughts of porn? Either the desire to view porn or thoughts of regret having done so?

8. Have you experienced sexual problems in your relationship such as difficulties experiencing orgasm or getting aroused?

9. Do you currently, or have you in the past, struggled with any other addiction or compulsive behaviour, such as drug or alcohol use, an eating disorder, gambling or gaming, or over work or exercise?

10. Has anyone in your family currently, or in the past, struggled with any addictions, compulsive behaviours or eating disorders such as those listed above?

If you answered 'yes' to more than half of these questions, then you almost certainly have some level of addiction. Your problem may be relatively mild at the moment, but it will most likely worsen if you don't stop now. If you answered 'yes' to most of the questions, then your addiction may already be firmly established – especially if you've been struggling like this for a number of years.

Ultimately, what defines porn use as an addiction, rather than a bad recreational habit, is the function that it serves. If you're viewing pornography purely as an aid to masturbation, say a few times a week for no more than 30 minutes at a time, then it's less likely to be an addiction. But if your viewing often extends to many hours at a time and you postpone reaching orgasm in order to extend your viewing for longer, then porn has become a means to escape something else. It has become what is often referred to as an anaesthetising behaviour.

All addictions are ways of escaping the pain of reality; they are a way of avoiding difficult emotions and problems in life. And hence, in order to beat the addiction, you need to find the truth behind what's causing it. What are you trying to escape from?

You may like to spend some time really thinking about that question. It is an important one to answer.

The truth behind the addiction

As we saw in Chapter 2, unfortunately some brains are more pre-disposed to addiction than others. If you have a parent who struggles with an addiction, then you will be more susceptible. We also know that people who come from families where there was separation, neglect or parental impairment are also more likely to become addicted. Anyone who has experienced a significant trauma also has a predisposition towards addiction. It used to be thought that trauma or attachment difficulties (the psychological term for parental difficulties in childhood) were at the root of all addictions, but since the advent of the internet, anyone can get addicted. Broadly speaking, the root of addiction can be described as attachment induced, trauma induced or opportunity induced. We will now look at each in turn.

ATTACHMENT INDUCED

Children need secure and reliable parenting in order to develop trusting relationships with others. When a child grows up knowing that they are loved and cared for, they are better equipped to manage whatever life may throw at them as they grow. Healthy attachment, as it is called, is a bit like the root system of a tree. If the roots are strong and deep, then the tree can withstand storms or drought, but a weak or shallow root system makes the tree vulnerable to being blown away and not developing healthy fruit. Safe, reliable, supportive parenting makes it possible for a child to make mistakes, learn from them and move on. But poor attachment means that addiction has a greater chance to take root and flourish.

Healthy attachment starts from the moment we are born. A baby needs to attach to their primary care giver, usually mum, to survive. A growing child continues to need that attachment in order to develop healthily. When they feel nurtured and cared for they have the courage to explore the world, knowing that safety is just a cry away. This attachment is important for emotional as well as physical development. When a child is too young to talk, they need a parent who is attuned to their needs and a parent who will be encouraging and responsive enough to help them develop the skills of communication. Without this, a child may not develop the necessary skills to identify and communicate their needs, nor to recognise and respond to the needs of others. This developmental impairment can result in becoming an adult who finds it difficult to trust that anyone can truly care for, or meet their needs, including their sexual needs. But the effects are not just emotional, they are also biologically imprinted. Research has shown that people with poor attachment are more likely to experience stress and anxiety, have weaker decision-making capacity and be at greater risk of addiction.

There are many different degrees of

unhealthy attachment. You may already know that your childhood was difficult and your problems stem from there. Or you may be aware that it was far from perfect and no doubt contributed in some way. But for others, the evidence of attachment difficulties comes from reflecting on how they relate to others as adults. For example, if you know that you are someone who tends to be very needy in relationships and in constant need of reassurance, then you may be what psychologists call an 'anxious attacher'. Or if you're or someone who finds it difficult to commit or find yourself quickly feeling suffocated in a relationship then you may be an 'avoidant attacher'. If you swing between the two, then you would be called an 'ambivalent attacher'.

You may also find the questions below helpful for considering if some of your issues stem from childhood.

1. Were you separated from your parents, for example through adoption, fostering, bereavement, or divorce?

2. Did you experience any significant periods of separation from your family, for example because of a parent's work or family illness, your own illness, or attending boarding school?

3. If there was no actual separation, were you often threatened with it? Perhaps if you were naughty or because a parent was often ill or your parents argued a lot?

4. Was your childhood overshadowed by an illness or disability, or a parent's addiction problem, domestic abuse, poverty or prejudice?

5. Did you grow up receiving little or no attention, affection or positive support and affirmation?

6. Were your relationships with friends difficult because of problems at home or because of a significant or regular house moves or schooling problems?

Most parents try to do their best, but we know that life can be messy and sometimes that means children do not receive the care and attention they need and deserve. The point of exploring this is not to blame parents, but to understand why you may be more susceptible to addiction and to help you recognise deeper areas of your life where you may need healing. We will look at that in more depth in the next chapter.

Real lives

Wayne had been brought up in a Christian home but like many young people, he felt restricted by what he saw as meaningless dogma and dropped out of church in his midteens. Around the same time, his sexuality was developing and with access to his own laptop, he discovered porn. He would have described his home as stable and loving, but much of his early years were spent being cared for by relatives as his younger brother had been born with a heart defect, which meant his parents spent a lot of time in hospital with him. When they were all together as a family, Wayne received little attention as his mother was frequently either exhausted or distracted by worry for his younger brother. He grew up learning to be independent and care for his own needs and as far as his parents were concerned, he was a perfect child. When Wayne discovered porn, he knew his parents and the church would disapprove, but by now he had got used to caring for himself and not relying on guidance from others. By the time he was 25 and reached out for help, his porn use had escalated to chatting to women online who gave him the undivided attention he had unconsciously craved all his life.

TRAUMA INDUCED

There are many different ways in which we can experience trauma; the most obvious are physical, sexual or emotional abuse. If you experienced any of these at the hands of someone you trusted, or your parents, then you may have a combination of an attachment and trauma induced addiction. But there are other forms of trauma too – ones that happen in childhood and those that happen later in life. For some, that's another type of physical or sexual assault, or verbal or physical bullying, ongoing experiences of humiliation or a significant loss through bereavement or an accident of some kind. For some, trauma has been a way of life, perhaps living in an environment where abuse was commonplace, though not directed at them, or taking a career in the forces, emergency services or health or social care where witnessing trauma is common.

Like attachment difficulties, the impact of trauma is both psychological and physiological. The impact will, of course, vary depending on the severity of the trauma, but most trauma survivors struggle with anxiety, anger and/or feelings of emptiness as a result. Some go on to become risk takers, as their psyche is so used to danger, and conversely, some become timid and fearful in the face of any kind of risk. The full impact of trauma can be hard to acknowledge because, as we said earlier, addiction is a powerful anaesthetic. Porn viewing or sexual acting out become a way of keeping the emotional pain of trauma at bay, so even if you say 'yes' to any of the following questions, you may be telling yourself that it's not that big a deal. But as we'll explore further in the next chapter, unless you're able to at least mentally recognise the trauma, then you will struggle to fully overcome your addiction.

1. Did you experience any kind of physical abuse in childhood, such as physical punishment from parents, siblings, carers, teachers or peers?
2. Did you experience ongoing threats of physical harm, or intimidation or verbal bullying – at any stage in your life?
3. Did you experience any form of sexual abuse, such as being touched inappropriately or being made to touch yourself or someone else? Or were you forced or encouraged to watch others being sexual or see explicit sexual material that made you feel uncomfortable, or at an age that you now know to be inappropriate?
4. Were you ever physically or sexually assaulted?
5. Were there ever any incidents of domestic violence in your home or times when you were fearful that someone was going to be hurt?

6. Did you experience any traumatic losses in your childhood or adolescence, for example bereavement, sudden disability or illness of someone close to you?

7. In adulthood, have you either been involved in any kind of trauma, such as an accident or sudden illness, or have you witnessed either of these (including in your work or ministry)?

8. In adulthood or adolescence did you experience any other significant shock to the system that left you feeling fearful for your safety or your future?

Real lives

Claire was a paediatric nurse working in intensive care, so witnessing trauma, both that of the children she nursed and their families, was part of her everyday life. She loved her job and regarded it as her Christian service, and when she initially sought help for porn addiction, she didn't think it was relevant. During conversation she shared that one of the reasons she had chosen her career was because she herself had spent much of her childhood in hospital after a playground accident had left her with a broken pelvis. Claire had chosen to remain celibate until she married her Christian husband but had already developed a porn habit before they met. She was sure she would stop when she started a sexual relationship, but with both her and her husband working in the medical profession, shift patterns often meant they barely spent any time together. Porn crept back in again as a way to express her sexuality, but she soon realised, that deep down, it was a way of soothing the anxiety and pain that accompanied her job and the unconscious memories they evoked.

OPPORTUNITY INDUCED ADDICTION

Now I know this is stating the obvious, but no one can become addicted to something unless there's the opportunity to do so. Pre-broadband, there were very few porn addicts and considerably fewer people who became addicted to other sexual activities. Not necessarily because they didn't want to, but simply because it was so much harder to access their drug of choice. In those days, most people who did develop a sexual addiction had a painful history and often a legacy of other addictive behaviours that they had regularly used to soothe their pain, but that is not the case today.

Technology has been a game changer when it comes to sex addiction. Not only does it provide easy, anonymous, free access, but it also delivers infinite variety. So, contrary to what some older books may tell you, not everyone who develops a porn or sex addiction has a difficult background. But let's face it, no parenting is perfect and in our fallen world, pain and suffering will inevitably touch us all. Sadly it's also true to say that most people, especially young people, will view porn at some stage, but only some go on to develop an addiction.

Below is a list of common areas that most people trapped by addiction have problems with. Take some time to read through each section and consider the ways in which you may struggle in each of these areas.

SELF CONTROL

We learn self-control from our parents, both from what they tell us and also from what we see. When parents tell children one thing, but then demonstrate another, they are more likely to grow up into adults who break, or bend, the rules. Boundaries are of course important for all of us, but so is choice. Many people who grew up in very strict environments, whether that's within the home or within a church community, struggle to make decisions for themselves.

They are so used to others holding the boundaries that they may struggle to set them for themselves, or they may resent authority and either overtly, or secretly rebel against it. Conversely, people who grew up in very relaxed, easy-going homes may have no experience of moderating their behaviour or considering the benefits of doing so.

EMOTIONAL REGULATION

Another essential lesson that parents need to teach is how to manage emotions. This side of heaven, we will all experience feelings of anger, frustration, disappointment, fear, loneliness, rejection, sadness and self-doubt at times –that's natural and normal. But if we don't know how to express these emotions in a healthy way, they can overwhelm us or feel like a weakness or a failing. Like the lessons in self-control, we learn from what our parents say, but also by what they do. If you've been told that anger is a sin, but grew up in a home where you frequently heard raised voices in arguments or witnessed passive aggressive behaviours such as getting the silent treatment, those mixed messages are going to cause a problem.

Perhaps one of the biggest mistakes that many well-meaning Christians make is to dismiss difficult emotions with the simple advice of trusting in God and handing our cares and woes to Him. This is of course excellent advice, but all of us need permission to be real, together with guidance and support on how we 'feel' as Christians. Many people I've worked with have long-standing struggles with anger and fear that are compounded by feelings of failure, guilt and shame, because they're not able to work through them or let them go.

SHAME

It's important to understand that shame and guilt are not the same. Guilt is a cognitive emotion that springs from our conscience when we have done something wrong and can be a motivator for positive change. Guilt is the voice in our head that says, "I did something bad". But shame is a much deeper, more wounding emotion that says, "I am bad". It is the self that becomes despised, rather than the wrongdoing.

Shame should also not be confused with spiritual conviction. When God convicts us of our sin we feel guilty and are called to turn to Him for His forgiveness and grace. Shame is akin to the devil's condemnation, where he accuses us of being a failure. Remember, "there is no condemnation in Christ Jesus" (see Romans 8:1).

Unfortunately, shame is common in the childhoods of people with sex and porn addiction and indeed common in Christians who struggle to experience the grace and forgiveness of God. For some, shame in childhood was inflicted from outside the family, perhaps in some form of social discrimination for race or religious reasons. For others, shame was used by parents as a tool for control and punishment, perhaps metered out in harsh critical statements, or silence, or humiliating punishments, rather than gentle correction.

SECRECY

All children are secretive – though many are not very good at it! Children will hide their toys, have secret imaginary friends and whisper secrets to friends in nursery. From a very young age, we are forming our individual identity and building bonds with others and one of the ways that we do that is by establishing areas of our life that are private from others and only shared with some. Secrets in themselves are not a problem, but when a child is brought up in a home where there are shameful secrets they have to keep, they may learn to keep secrets for the wrong reasons. For some, the secret may be something serious such as abuse of themselves or another family member. Or there may be family secrets such as on-going marriage problems, infidelity, a parent's addiction or mental health problem, domestic violence, a wayward sibling or debt. In these families there may be a public front of decency and order and the child may quickly learn to maintain this pretence. Unfortunately this can set up a pattern of behaviour where double standards, or even a double life, are the norm.

SEX EDUCATION

Poor or limited sex education is common in people who develop porn or sex addiction. Some may only have learnt the dangers of sex and been left alone to discover its pleasures, whereas others may have been brought up with vague or abusive sexual boundaries where they failed to learn the benefits of moderation. We talked about the role of shame in the development of addiction earlier, but when that shame is linked to sexuality, then some kind of sexual behaviour is more likely to be chosen as the 'drug' of choice.

In Chapter 1 we explored what healthy sexuality might mean to Christians – if you've skipped that chapter, it might be worth going back to look at it now to help you consider what you learnt about sex as you were growing up.

Adolescence is a critical time for identity development and also the time when most people are discovering their sexual selves. It's also the time when 'fitting in' with your peers is most important. Children transition into adulthood by looking to peers for guidance and affirmation, rather than parents.

In the research I undertook for my *Understanding and Treating Sex Addiction* book, 64% of people with sex addiction said they often felt they didn't 'fit in' during adolescence and 1 in 5 said that adolescent isolation was the most influential factor in developing their addiction. There are many reasons why that might happen. For some it's the wrong trainers or haircut, for others it's not fitting in academically or in sport. Another common reason is frequent school changes or home moves or being a member of a family that is in some way different from others. Whatever the reason, shyness or social anxiety often develop and make it more likely that masturbation and porn will become a place of solace.

Real lives

Khalid was 37 when he came for help with porn addiction. His parents had moved to the UK from the Middle East when he was four years old and he described his family as strict, but always loving and secure. They lived in a predominantly white suburb of London and as his mother and sisters continued to wear the traditional Middle Eastern head dress,

Khalid had always felt different from others. He worked hard to fit in, but even in the new church that his family joined in his early teens, he was acutely aware that they were different. Khalid was also brought up with secrets; his parents often talked in hushed tones about the country they'd left behind, but refused to tell any of the children what had happened. In his teens, Khalid became increasingly angry that he was not trusted to know more about his past, but anger was not allowed in his family and seen as disrespectful. Masturbating to porn in his room soon became a way of both soothing his anger and quietly rebelling against his family's value system, but over time, developed into a shameful, isolating secret life.

HOW DID YOU REACT WHEN YOU READ KHALID'S STORY?

DO YOU KNOW HOW IT FEELS TO LEAD A SHAME-FILLED, ISOLATING AND SECRET EXISTENCE?

COULD YOU DESCRIBE YOURSELF AS SOMEONE WITH A 'DOUBLE-LIFE'?

Hopefully reading this chapter has given you more of an insight into your problem with porn and whether or not it has developed into an addiction. The next two chapters are devoted to guidance on how to overcome it.

Reflection

In this chapter we have explored:

- Why breaking through denial is so important
- The harmful consequences caused by porn
- How to know if you're 'addicted' to porn
- Some common underlying causes of addiction

Before we end this chapter you might want to take a few moments to reflect on these amazing verses taken from Psalm 51 (NLT). Often referred to as "The Sinner's Prayer", they were written by David in the aftermath of his sexual sin with Bathsheba.

YOU MAY LIKE TO UNDERLINE THE VERSES THAT RESONATE MOST.

IN WHAT WAYS DO YOU RELATE TO THESE WORDS?

WHY DID YOU UNDERLINE THOSE WORDS IN PARTICULAR?

Have mercy on me, O God, because of your unfailing love. Because of your great compassion, blot out the stain of my sins.

Wash me clean from my guilt. Purify me from my sin. For I recognize my rebellion; it haunts me day and night.

Against you, and you alone, have I sinned; I have done what is evil in your sight. You will be proved right in what you say, and your judgment against me is just.

For I was born a sinner—yes, from the moment my mother conceived me. But you desire honesty from the womb, teaching me wisdom even there.

Purify me from my sins, and I will be clean; wash me, and I will be whiter than snow. Oh, give me back my joy again; you have broken me — now let me rejoice. Don't keep looking at my sins. Remove the stain of my guilt.

Create in me a clean heart, O God. Renew a loyal spirit within me. Do not banish me from your presence, and don't take your Holy Spirit from me. Restore to me the joy of your salvation, and make me willing to obey you.

You do not desire a sacrifice, or I would offer one. You do not want a burnt offering. The sacrifice you desire is a broken spirit. You will not reject a broken and repentant heart, O God.

Now that you've thought more about your own life and how it could have been affected by porn, you can use the exercise below to boost your motivation and commitment to quit. It allows you to compare the pros and cons of continuing to view porn and then the pros and cons of quitting. As you fill in the boxes, think about the practical, physical, emotional and spiritual impact on you and also on others you care about.

IF I CONTINUE VIEWING PORN

BENEFITS / PROS	COSTS / CONS

IF I STOP VIEWING PORN

BENEFITS / PROS	COSTS / CONS

DID ANYTHING SURPRISE YOU ABOUT THAT EXERCISE?

WHAT DID YOU LEARN ABOUT YOURSELF OR YOUR SITUATION THAT YOU WERE NOT FULLY AWARE OF BEFORE?

HOW HAS THAT MADE YOU FEEL?

REMEMBER THAT WE SAID EARLIER, GUILT IS THE VOICE IN OUR HEAD THAT SAYS, "I DID SOMETHING BAD". BUT SHAME IS A MUCH DEEPER, MORE WOUNDING EMOTION THAT SAYS, "I AM BAD". MAKE SURE YOU ARE TUNING IN TO THE RIGHT VOICE HERE.

YOU MAY LIKE TO WRITE A PRAYER, ASKING GOD TO HELP YOU WITH ANY DECISIONS YOU NEED TO MAKE.

CHAPTER FOUR

Understanding the cycle of addiction

"I do not understand what I do. For what I want to do, I do not do, but what I hate I do."
(ROMANS 7:15 NIV)

When it comes to compulsive behaviours, we do what we don't want to do because we get trapped in the cycle of addiction. The addiction cycle is exhausting and can feel endless. Constantly fluctuating between commitment to change and the pain of failure, over time we can become increasingly convinced that perhaps change is impossible for us. But I can absolutely assure you that change is possible. You cannot control the cycle of addiction, but you can get off it. This chapter will give you what you need to identify your cycle and get off it, for good.

Below is the six-phase cycle that I have developed over years of helping people through addiction. It enables clients to understand and recognise how, and why, their addiction continues to maintain itself through their behaviours, thoughts and emotions. The length of each phase, and the length of time between each phase, varies from person to person - as does the content. But, if you are an addict, you will find yourself easily able to identify with the cycle.

The six-phase cycle

- **The dormant phase** - this is when life 'appears' normal and perhaps you're not struggling with porn at all, but it's temporary and it's only a matter of time before something 'triggers' you into your unwanted behaviours again. For some this may be months, even years – for others it's just a few days.

- **The trigger phase** – a trigger is an emotion, event or opportunity that makes you want to 'act out'. For some it's related to stress or anxiety, for others it's feeling depressed or lonely, but for many it's simply having the opportunity. There may be one trigger, but often it's a series of triggers that build over time.

- **The preparation phase** - the preparation phase varies in length considerably, but this is the time when the internal thought battle is going on that you inevitably lose. You know you shouldn't, but you're coming up with reasons why you will. For some this goes on for days, for others just a few moments. Depending on the acting out behaviour, this might also include practical strategies for creating the opportunity to act out.

- **The acting out phase** – this may mean watching porn just for one sitting or a period of binging over many days. Or, if your behaviours have escalated beyond viewing porn, it might be chatting and flirting, on or offline, or meeting up with someone for sex.

- **The regret phase** – depending on the consequences of acting out and how hard you've been trying to stop, the regret phase may be little more than disappointment at giving in to temptation again, or it may be weeks of shame, despair, depression and beating yourself up.

- **The reconstruction phase** – this is the phase when you're trying to put yourself and your life back together again. It might mean confession and prayer, sharing with someone else, commitments to stop and renewed efforts at previous relapse prevention strategies. But, until you've really understood your cycle and what's at the root of your problem, you'll just be going back into the dormant phase, waiting for the inevitable trigger to happen again.

Understanding the cycle and personalising it gives you the opportunity to break it and end it. We'll look in more depth at each phase now and you'll find some questions to help you consider exactly what is happening for you in each phase.

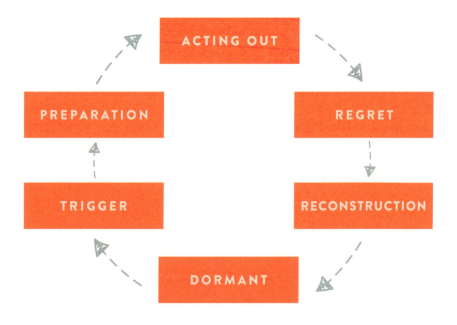

The dormant phase

The dormant phase is sometimes the hardest for people to understand. Assuming you're reading this book in order, and haven't skipped chapter four, you may already have an idea of whether or not your addiction is attachment, trauma or opportunity induced. And if you've read through the list of common underlying causes, you may already know that some of those apply to you. For example, if you know that you sometimes struggle to regulate your emotions, in the dormant phase those difficulties are still there, but nothing is happening in your life that you're emotionally struggling with. But until you develop the skills of healthy emotional regulation, you will be at risk of being triggered into watching porn again. If you're still carrying the wounds of trauma, whether that's abuse, assault or a sudden loss, then you will still be vulnerable to triggers that make you feel anxious, depressed or empty inside. Those who had unreliable parenting or another significant relationship difficulty that has not been addressed, will continue to be vulnerable to turning to porn for comfort when they feel lonely, rejected or overwhelmed by the needs of others. The following list of questions can help you to consider what might be going on for you beneath your addiction.

1. Do you struggle to trust other people in your life?
   YES   NO   MAYBE
2. Do you often feel overwhelmed by other people's demands?
   YES   NO   MAYBE
3. Do you find it difficult to healthily express and manage anger?
   YES   NO   MAYBE
4. Do you struggle with anxiety or depression?
   YES   NO   MAYBE
5. Do you often feel as though you don't really fit in or that you're not the same as other people?
   YES   NO   MAYBE

6. Do you struggle to feel close to God?
   YES   NO   MAYBE
7. Do you find it hard to believe, at a heart level, that God loves you?
   YES   NO   MAYBE
8. Do you often compare yourself to others and fear you're not as good as they are?
   YES   NO   MAYBE
9. Do you feel as though no one is really there for you?
   YES   NO   MAYBE
10. Do you find it difficult to be alone?
    YES   NO   MAYBE
11. Do you find yourself getting tense when you're not busy?
    YES   NO   MAYBE
12. Do you struggle with boredom?
    YES   NO   MAYBE
13. Do you love yourself?
    YES   NO   MAYBE
14. Are you able to see yourself through God's eyes?
    YES   NO   MAYBE
15. Do you struggle with feelings of resentment towards others and maybe God?
    YES   NO   MAYBE
16. Do you feel as though you're not appreciated for what you do?
    YES   NO   MAYBE
17. Do you worry about what people think of you and easily feel rejected?
    YES   NO   MAYBE
18. Do you struggle to believe in God's provision for you, now or in the future?
    YES   NO   MAYBE

19. Do you feel in your heart, that your sins are unforgiveable?
YES   NO   MAYBE

20. Do you harbour unforgiveness in your heart?
YES   NO   MAYBE

Whatever you've answered 'yes' to, needs to be resolved. For some, that might simply mean more prayer and Bible study, for others it might mean talking to someone, a friend, pastor or counsellor. However, if this is something that you've been struggling with for some time, then chances are your compulsive behaviour has become a way of managing it. And whilst porn might work as a quick fix, it's not resolving the problem deep down. Furthermore, your continuing porn use is going to cause even more difficulties that you're going to need to escape from.

As we've said before, ultimately addiction is an anaesthetising behaviour. It's a way of managing difficult emotions, both past and present, and until you can either resolve your difficulties or find better ways of managing them, you'll continue to be at risk of acting out again. If you're still struggling to find what might be happening for you in the dormant phase, you might like to try the Fruits of the Spirit exercise in Chapter 7.

The trigger phase

Broadly speaking, triggers are either environmental or emotional. In other words, you either find yourself with what feels like an irresistible opportunity to act out, or you are emotionally overwhelmed by a sudden event, or emotionally worn down by a series of events.

The word that many Christians might use for triggers is 'temptations'. The Christian life does not promise to be one without temptation. Indeed, many would say that the temptations are magnified, as we get closer to God. The Bible makes it clear that we are in the midst of spiritual warfare. In Ephesians 6:12, Paul says that we must wrestle, 'against, principalities, against powers, against the rulers of the darkness of this world, against spiritual wickedness in high places' (NKJV).

Many Christians confuse temptation with sin, but that is the devil's scheme to discourage us and blame us whenever we're tempted. Sexual temptation is not a sin, though of course, giving in to it is. Jesus himself was tempted, but He did not allow himself to be condemned for it (See Hebrews 4:15). All Christians struggle with sexual temptation, it's how you manage it that matters. We will explore more of this later in this chapter.

But having said all that, the Bible is also clear that we should not flirt with temptation - we should not deliberately put ourselves in the devil's firing line. Proverbs is full of advice for healthy living and tells us through many different metaphors to avoid foolish ways and choose the way of wisdom. The wise way is to avoid temptation, whenever you can. Below is an exercise to help you identify areas that could be triggering and tempting to you. You may not be able to avoid all of them, but identify the ones you can. In the next chapter we will explore how to manage the triggers that you can't.

IDENTIFYING TRIGGERS

Below is a list of the five most common areas where people find themselves triggered. Read the following and then take a piece of paper and write down your most common triggers. Think about times in the past and also imagine situations in the future that you know you would find difficult.

- **People** – for example, non-Christian friends and/or colleagues, Christian friends that you envy because they don't struggle with this (as far as you know!). A triggering person may be your partner, or a work colleague or particular people that irritate you or that you are envious of. Like many, you might find yourself triggered by sexually attractive people, either in your everyday world or on television or in films.
- **Places** – this might include particular places where you've acted out before, such as your home or your office. Or it may be particular locations such as when you're away staying in hotels. There may also be places that trigger you where you know there will be attractive people, such as at the beach or the gym or bars and nightclubs.
- **Events** – events and places may be similar, so don't worry if you've put some things in the category above, but here I'm meaning things like, when you're alone at home or when the office is empty. Or perhaps when you go to a party or there's another celebratory event. Or it may be something very specific to you, such as struggling when you have to do a particular task or perhaps when you have an argument with someone. Or it may occur when your partner seems distant from you. If you're a woman struggling with addiction, then you might notice that you're more triggered at certain times of the month and also when you're getting dressed up for a night out or painting your nails or moisturising your body.
- **Feelings** – this is the biggest category and it includes all the emotions that you struggle with, such as feeling angry, lonely, resentful, depressed, anxious or stressed. For some, positive emotions can also be a trigger, such as when you feel you want to celebrate or deserve a reward. Sexual desire is of course another common trigger, not really a 'feeling', but

something to make a note of here. Many female addicts notice that they're susceptible to triggers when they're feeling 'sexy.'

- **Thoughts** - you might be aware that certain thinking patterns also trigger you - such as feeling sorry for yourself or beating yourself up, or perhaps thinking that acting out won't really do any harm. There's more on thinking patterns in the next section too.

Once you've written your own list, have a look at which ones you could avoid. Not necessarily for the rest of your life, but at least for the next few months while you're giving up porn. So if the gym is a trigger for you, perhaps you don't want to rule that out for the rest of your life, but you could take up running alone for a while and only go back to the gym when you're stronger in your recovery. Or there may be particular people that you could avoid now or television programmes that should be off your viewing list. Emotions are of course harder to avoid, but if stress is a trigger for you, then consider ways you can reduce your stress while you're getting into recovery. There's much more in the next chapter on how to manage triggers.

The preparation phase

Once triggered, the addiction enters the preparation phase of the cycle and, whether consciously, or unconsciously, you'll be making the necessary practical and psychological arrangements to act out.

For many people, this preparation phase is also part of the buzz. For some that might be working out how to get round the latest porn blocking software on the computer or manipulating a situation where they'll have time alone to get online. Or if your behaviour has escalated beyond porn, you might be researching potential partners online or updating your online profile. Or perhaps squirrelling away secret sums of money to pay for a visit to a massage parlour or visit a sex worker. Dopamine is beginning to pump round the brain as the anticipation builds and the promise of reward grows stronger. As we saw in Chapter 2, sex and porn addiction has very little to do with sexual satiation, it's about the anticipation of reward and the opportunity to escape real life.

But the preparation phase is also the time when the battle within your head and heart begins to rage - the proverbial angel on one shoulder and devil on the other. The internal conflict heightens as your conscience says "No," but your increasing dopamine levels shout "Yes!" Everyone with an addiction develops a range of what we call 'cognitive distortions' that gives them the excuse to act out. As Christians, we might call them the devil's lies, many of which are extremely cunning and convincing. When you can recognise those lies for what they really are, then you'll be in a stronger position to denounce them. Here's a list of common cognitive distortions.

COMMON COGNITIVE DISTORTIONS

1. I'm already doomed (futility)
2. All men/women do this (normalising)
3. It's not my fault (blaming)
4. I'm just too weak (being a victim)
5. I deserve this (entitlement)

6. It's not as bad as another sin (minimisation)
7. I couldn't help it (I was drunk, I was depressed - excuses)
8. Someone else does it (comparison)

These may not be your exact words, but you may be able to relate to the sentiment behind them. But we know this is not the TRUTH!

Write down what lies you hear and fall for – and next time you hear that voice in your head saying them, remember them for what they are; the devil's scheme to make you feel shame and try and separate you from your Father.

Let's look at what the Bible says about these distortions and how it offers us the real picture of what God thinks of us.

1. If we are tempted to say, "I'm already doomed" we can read this promise from 2 Peter 1:4 (NLT)

> *"And because of his glory and excellence, he has given us great and precious promises. These are the promises that enable you to share his divine nature and escape the world's corruption caused by human desires."*

Or this verse from Isaiah 41:10 (NIV)

> *"Fear not, for I am with you; be not dismayed, for I am your God; I will strengthen you, I will help you, I will uphold you with my righteous right hand."*

And this wonderful verse from Jeremiah 29:11 (NLT)

> *"For I know the plans I have for you", says the Lord. "They are plans for good and not for disaster, to give you a future and a hope."*

2. If we are tempted to say, "All men do this" we can declare the truth from 1 Peter 1:16 (NIV)

> *"For it is written: "Be holy, because I am holy."*

And these comforting words from Isaiah 40:29-31 (NLT)

> *"He gives power to the weak and strength to the powerless. Even youths will become weak and tired, and young men will fall in exhaustion. But those who trust in the Lord will find new strength. They will soar high on wings like eagles. They will run and not grow weary. They will walk and not faint."*

3. If we are tempted to say, "It's not my fault" we can remind ourselves of the powerful truth of 1 John 1:8-9 (ESV) which says,

> *"If we say we have no sin, we deceive ourselves, and the truth is not in us. If we confess our sins, he is faithful and just to forgive us our sins and to cleanse us from all unrighteousness."*

4. If we are saying, "I am too weak," we can speak out the power of Matthew 11:28-29 (NLT)

> *"Then Jesus said, "Come to me, all of you who are weary and carry heavy burdens, and I will give you rest. Take my yoke upon you. Let me teach you, because I am humble and gentle at heart, and you will find rest for your ouls. For my yoke is easy to bear, and the burden I give you is light."*

5. If we find ourselves saying, "I deserve or need this" we can speak out the truth from Philippians 4:19 (NLT)

> *"And this same God who takes care of me will supply all your needs from his glorious riches, which have been given to us in Christ Jesus."*

6. If we lie to ourselves and say it is "not as bad as another sin," we need to hear the truth of Matthew 7:3 (NIV)

> *"Why do you look at the speck of sawdust in your brother's eye and pay no attention to the plank in your own eye?"*

And Romans 3:23 (NIV)

> *"...for all have sinned and fall short of the glory of God."*

7. If we say, "I couldn't help it" we need to hear the power of Romans 14:12 (AMP) which says,

> *"So then each of us shall give account of himself to God."*

And the comfort of Proverbs 1:33 (NLT)

> *"But all who listen to me will live in peace, untroubled by fear of harm."*

8. If we hear ourselves speaking that "others sin," we need to say the verse from James 4:17 (NLT)

> *"Remember, it is sin to know what you ought to do and then not do it.*

> *"No, despite all these things, overwhelming victory is ours through Christ, who loved us."*
> *Romans 8:37 (NLT)*

The acting out phase

The term 'acting out' is used to describe whatever your sexual behaviour might be. For most it's porn, but it may have escalated to other behaviours as well. As we've said before, all addictions serve the function of avoiding some kind of emotional pain, whether that's a result of childhood difficulties, trauma, relationship problems or struggles to handle emotions healthily. And of course, the first pain that acting out soothes is the craving to act out.

Below is an exercise that can help you to identify what you're really getting from acting out. No doubt there is sexual excitement, but what else? Once you can identify the deeper emotional needs you'll be in a stronger position to find alternative ways of getting these needs met. If you act out in a variety of ways, for example watching porn and also multiple affairs, then you may notice that you experience different benefits from each activity.

EMOTIONAL BENEFITS OF ACTING OUT

Relaxation
Invigoration
Calmness
Affirmation
Connection with others
Feeling valued
Feeling wanted
A sense of reward
Excitement
Autonomy
Powerful
In control

Typically, people with an attachment induced addiction will feel valued, wanted, connected and/or autonomous, whereas those with a trauma induced addiction will feel in control, calm or invigorated. Sometimes identifying the benefits will give you more clues to what's going on for you in the dormant phase, that you need to address. Some people experience the benefits within minutes of acting out, whilst others will binge for days before these deeper needs are fulfilled. Either way, once it's over, you will enter the regret phase.

The regret phase

Most Christians feel bitter regret and shame after acting out because the behavours are so opposed to their value system. Furthermore, many feel hugely isolated from loved ones as the secrecy and shame of the behaviour leaves them unable to feel fully known and loved. For women who struggle with addictive sexual behaviours, the feelings of shame can be even greater. Our culture assumes that men have the higher sex drives and are drawn to pornography, but when women struggle in these areas they are often not believed or deemed to be a 'slut'. This can make it even harder for women to reach out for help.

For those who have been discovered, the regret is accompanied by even greater shame and remorse as they witness the pain their behaviour has on others. The extent of regret and the length of the phase depends on what the behaviour has been and the consequences, but most want to escape this phase as quickly as possible and get back to normal again.

The reconstruction phase

Basically this phase is where someone with an addiction takes active steps to put their life back together again. That may include practical strategies such as installing porn blocking software and deleting social media accounts. It may also include recommitting to a regular routine of physical exercise, putting dates in the diary to visit friends or renewing efforts to spend more time with a spouse and family. For Christians, this may also include increasing spiritual activities such as prayer and Bible study and perhaps confessing to those in spiritual leadership and asking for prayer. Those voices in your head will also be busy again reminding you of what you've done and telling you that you'll never do it again.

As with the other phases, the length of time varies. For some it's just a few hours, for others it's days or even months before life feels back to normal. But it's the false 'pretend normal' of the dormant phase, where the underlying issues remain unresolved and often unacknowledged, and the same vulnerability remains, waiting for the next trigger.

Below are two real life stories of people who have identified the phases in their addiction cycle. I hope that reading these will help you to see how each phase links with the other.

Michael's cycle of addiction

Michael was 52 years old and had been a senior pastor in a free church for nearly 20 years. His secret addiction to pornography had started in his teens, before he came to faith, and although he'd had long periods of abstinence, the problem had escalated over recent years to online webcam sex. Michael was able to recognise that in his dormant phase there were many unresolved issues linked to his childhood. In many ways, he'd always been in the position of pastor; as the eldest of 5 children he had been brought up in a family where his father's temper frequently resulted in violence towards his mother and the children. His role in the family became protector of his younger siblings, confidant to his mother and peace keeper to his father. He never learnt to express his needs for care, but instead, cared for others, with varying levels of reward and resentment. Michael's most common triggers were when he was feeling overburdened by other's need, which often happened in his busy Church, or when his wife or children became angry. He recognised that he had no mechanism for managing his own anger, and hence any frustrating situation or perceived attack from another, could be a trigger. In the preparation phase he would tell himself that he deserved something for himself and having spent so many years listening to the confessions of other Christians, he would comfort himself with the knowledge that what he was doing wasn't as bad as others. He also knew that God would forgive him and reasoned that his times of weakness helped him have more empathy with others. When he acted out with pornography, his anger was soothed and he felt calm and relaxed. And when he met a sex worker on webcam, he felt wanted, affirmed and rewarded. But in the regret phase, Michael hated himself. He had betrayed his wife and the trust of his congregation. He felt like a hypocrite and in the reconstruction phase he would double his efforts to care for the needs of others and serve sacrificially. But sadly this just fed his inability to care for himself and resolve his dormant issues. So it was only a matter of time before he would be triggered, by feeling overburdened or frustrated again.

Francis' cycle of addiction

Francis was a 22-year-old medical student and a porn addict. He had been brought up in a strict Presbyterian family and Church and had never smoked, drunk or tried any kind of illegal drugs. He'd also never had a girlfriend, as he wanted no distractions while he was studying for his future career as a surgeon. Initially, Francis had no idea why or how porn had hooked him so badly. He had never seen pornography until his first year at University where his fellow housemates, all of whom viewed regularly, introduced him to the idea. He said it had started purely out of curiosity, but he soon discovered it was a very effective way of relieving exam and study stress and his usage had grown significantly over the past four years. It was easier for Francis to recognise the triggers – it was always linked to stress – but by digging a little deeper he recognised that he struggled with profound fears of inadequacy and failure. His father was a hospital doctor and had encouraged Francis to "succeed where he had failed." As a very bright and gifted child, he had been encouraged to work hard and reach, what his parents called, his God given potential. In Francis' dormant phase were his unspoken fears of disappointing his family, and his God. University was tougher than he thought, so feeling inadequate and stressed were common triggers. In the preparation phase he would tell himself that it was ok to look at porn because all lads do, and it's not as bad as alcohol, drugs or sleeping around – things all the other lads also seemed to do. But afterwards his regret phase was full of shame and self-recriminations for failing to control himself and increasing fear that the time he'd wasted should have been spent on study. The reconstruction phase was spent praying and fasting and putting more porn blocks on his computer that hopefully he wouldn't be able to get around. But the weeks of dormancy dragged fearfully by until the next essay deadline triggered him back online.

Reflection

In this chapter we have:

1. Explored how addictive behaviours get trapped in a cycle
2. Looked at the lies the enemy tells us about ourselves
3. Explored exercises to help us identify the dormant, trigger, preparation, acting out, regret and reconstitution phases of our cycles.

WHAT NEW THINGS HAVE YOU DISCOVERED OR REMEMBERED ABOUT YOURSELF?

HAS ANYTHING SURPRISED OR SHOCKED YOU?

HOW CAN THAT IMPACT YOUR RECOVERY?

WHO CAN YOU SHARE YOUR JOURNEY WITH?

Many people find it valuable to write down how they feel as a way of journaling their progress and understanding themselves more fully. Perhaps you could start such a journal today?

Take a look at these encouraging verses from Romans 8:33-34 (NLT)

"Who dares accuse us whom God has chosen for his own? No one—for God himself has given us right standing with himself. Who then will condemn us? No one—for Christ Jesus died for us and was raised to life for us, and he is sitting in the place of honor at God's right hand, pleading for us."

Turn your thoughts about these verses into a prayer, thanking God that he knows your every weakness, but, beautifully chooses not to condemn you.

Remind yourself that Jesus himself is pleading for you.

You may like to use the blank areas in the diagram to personalise the key points you have learned about your cycle of addiction.

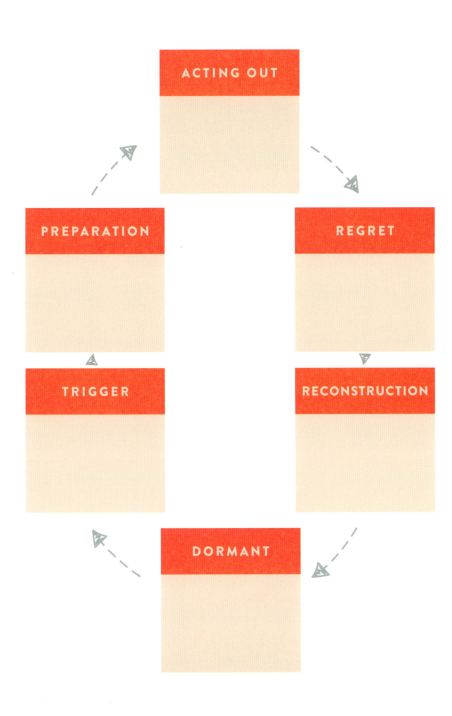

CHAPTER FIVE

Finding freedom

This chapter is devoted to helping you overcome your addiction. It is my hope, that there will be sufficient information here to get you firmly on the road to recovery. We will be covering the 'holy trinity' of recovery – the three pillars that you will need in order to step into freedom from porn addiction. Each is dependent on the others and none will work alone.

These are the 3 pillars of recovery:

1. Accountability
2. Relapse prevention
3. Change your life

We'll look at each in more detail in a moment, but first let me explain why each is so important and how they intertwine with each other.

Accountability to at least one other person, preferably more, is essential to recovery. Without this, it is easy to slip and slide back into addiction without anyone knowing. Accountability also provides support and challenge while you establish relapse prevention strategies as well as during the work you undergo to change your lifestyle.

Relapse prevention will give you the practical strategies to change your behaviours, but unless you also work on the underlying causes and create a new way of living for yourself, you will find it an almost impossibly hard slog. What's more, whilst you may stop your problems with porn, there's a risk that you'll adopt other unhelpful behaviours to manage those unresolved issues.

Changing your life is undoubtedly the most important pillar. That means developing a lifestyle that no longer needs addiction. A life that is spiritually, physically and emotionally healthy; a life that is fulfilled and connected; and free of shame. Whilst it may be possible to do that without anyone knowing the reason why, and establish relapse prevention strategies to keep you safe, we were not created to walk our lives alone.

Accountability

Addiction thrives in secrecy and shame and the most effective way of counteracting that is to step out of the shadows and into the light. Proverbs 28:13 (NASB) says,

> *"He who conceals his transgressions will not prosper, but he who confesses and forsakes them will find compassion."*

Sharing with others allows us to be truly known, accepted and loved for who we are. True fellowship with others is not possible while we continue to hide.

1 John 1: 17 (ESV) says,

> *"But if we walk in the Light as He Himself is in the Light, we have fellowship with one another, and the blood of Jesus His Son cleanses us from all sin."*

Furthermore, if you're part of a recovery community, you will see that you are not alone with this problem and witness first hand how this addiction can affect anyone. As you experience empathy and compassion for them, the shame you feel will slip away. Jesus said, "Do not judge, and you will not be judged; and do not condemn, and you will not be condemned; pardon, and you will be pardoned. Give, and it will be given to you. They will pour into your lap a good measure, pressed down, shaken together, and running over. For by your standard of measure, it will be measured to you in return." (Luke 6:37-38 NASB). There is nowhere, but in the company of others, that you can experience the promise of these verses.

What's more, the recovery journey is often a long one, and the support of others will not only keep you on track, but also provide essential encouragement when you struggle. It says in Ecclesiastes 4:9-12 (NLT), "Two people are better off than one, for they can help each other succeed. If one person falls, the other can reach out and help. But someone who falls alone is in real trouble. Likewise, two people lying close together can keep each other warm. But how can one be warm alone? A person standing alone can be attacked and defeated, but two can stand back-to-back and conquer. Three are even better, for a triple-braided cord is not easily broken."

The wisdom of this verse says that you will benefit from confiding in at least two people, personally I think three is even better (a triple-braided cord is not easily broken). We'll look now at who those people may be.

WHO TO SHARE WITH

If you're in a relationship, and you want your relationship to be happy and fulfilled, then you need to tell your partner. Now I totally understand that some people reading that last line will be saying "What? If my partner knew, there is no way our relationship would be happy and fulfilled!" As we said earlier in this chapter, addiction thrives in secrecy and shame and all the while your partner does not know what you're struggling with, not only will they not be able to support you, but you will never be able to feel confident in their love for you. Also, all the time you hold a secret, that secret will damage the intimacy between you. There isn't space to talk about this fully within this book, but if your partner doesn't know, you should consider making a 'disclosure'. There is a right and a wrong way to disclose and there are harmful details that are unnecessary to disclose. So before you proceed, please do read my other book, 'Sex Addiction – The Partner's Perspective', where I talk in depth about the disclosure process. Or, speak to a trained professional who is experienced in this field.

In addition to your partner (if you have one), I would still recommend three other accountability partners. Whilst your partner can be an essential source of support to you, this is not the person who you should turn to every time you are struggling. As I have said earlier in this book, many partners find sex or porn addiction traumatic and this means that sharing ongoing struggles can unnecessarily add to that trauma. It is important that you are honest about your recovery, but ongoing support needs to come from people who are able to be less emotionally involved. The road to recovery will include temptations, which may be insensitive to share with a partner, but the journey will also include many victories. But understandably, many people find it difficult to share those victories and congratulate their partners for what, to most, would simply equate to 'normal' marriage requirements. In other words, don't expect your partner to praise you for not looking at porn or for not having sex outside of your marriage! But please do find someone who will.

When looking for others to share your journey with, consider friends, family members, church leaders, pastoral carers, small group members, therapists, online recovery forums and/or recovery groups. Ideally, there should be at least one person who is within your church community who can support you spiritually, one person who is in recovery themselves where you can encourage and challenge each other, and someone who is trained in addiction recovery who can guide you and ensure you're on the right path.

I have been running groups for people in recovery for many years, and I can bear witness to the fact that these are significantly more successful than individual therapy or people who try and go it alone. God created us for community and that's why a recovery community, whatever shape that takes, is so successful. You'll find more information on what's available in Chapter 7.

Relapse prevention

Now we're getting to the nitty-gritty stuff of recovery. I want to help you to develop a set of strategies to avoid your triggers and manage the unavoidable ones. In this section you'll also find some guidance on managing one of the most common relapse triggers which is sexual urges. But first, let's explore what relapse means and how it happens.

UNDERSTANDING RELAPSE

One of the biggest mistakes that people make in recovery is thinking that relapse is a one-off event that happens, rather than a process that evolves. There are three stages to relapse.

First is 'emotional relapse' and you can recognise this when you find yourself struggling with stress, frustration or low self-esteem. It will feel as though all those old emotional wounds are opening up again. As we've said before, God does not promise us a pain-free existence – life is full of struggles and for someone with an addiction, times of struggle make them vulnerable to triggers. Earlier in the book, we looked at the importance of resolving issues in the 'dormant phase' and we'll explore this further later in this chapter too.

The second stage of relapse is 'mental relapse'. This is when the desire to act out starts creeping into your awareness and those old cognitive distortions from the devil start battling in your head.

And the final stage is 'physical relapse' – in other words, you've done it again! By heeding the signs of an emotional relapse and getting back on track, you can avoid the anguish of the mental relapse and the almost inevitable physical relapse. But if you do find yourself in the final stage, all is not lost.

It's an unfortunate reality that many people with addiction will at times 'slip' but that doesn't mean you have to experience a full relapse. A 'slip' can be helpfully described by an acronym, as a:

SHORT
LAPSE
IN
PROGRESS.

For example, watching raunchy YouTube clips or staying up late to watch an erotic film which you know is not OK for you. Or it may be 'window shopping' on a dating site or sex worker site, sending a flirtatious text or lusting with your eyes. Now I'm not saying that any of this is OK, but it is important to distinguish this from a full relapse and going back to all your old behaviours. If you don't, then you're likely to become discouraged and fall for the cognitive distortion "I've already blown it so I might as well go all the way." Whether you 'slip', or relapse, get back on track immediately. Never forget that the "one who is in you is greater than the one who is in the world." (1 John 4:4 NIV).

AVOID TRIGGERS

In the last chapter there was an exercise on identifying triggers. If you haven't already completed that, you will find it useful to do it now. Avoiding triggers is not always possible, but once you know what they are, you can make plans to avoid them. One of the key elements of relapse prevention is planning. There's a common cliché, 'Failing to prepare is preparing to fail', and like many clichés, it's irritating, because it's right! So look back at the list of triggers you have identified and take steps to avoid them. In addition, below are a few other essentials.

- **Spiritual protection** – Matthew 26:41 (NKJV) says "Watch and pray, lest you enter into temptation. The spirit indeed is willing, but the flesh is weak." As a Christian, this has to be your number one relapse prevention strategy: regular, ongoing prayer and communion with your Father and members of your Christian community. If you don't want to be a lost sheep or get eaten by a wolf, stay close to your shepherd and in the fold. There are ideas for spiritual exercises, Bible readings and other good books to read in the following chapter.

- **Opportunity protection** – if you don't have a diary, get one and plan every week in advance. Consider where you might be vulnerable and take alternative action. For example, if you're at risk when you're alone in the house, make arrangements to visit friends or go to the cinema. If there's an event coming up that could be triggering, ask someone to go with you or cancel. If that's impossible, at least ensure that you're driving so there's no temptation to reduce your inhibitions with alcohol. In the early stages of recovery, keep busy. There's an old English saying "The devil makes work for idle hands." Although it's not a direct quote from the Bible, there is plenty of advice in Proverbs and from Paul about the importance of using our time productively. That doesn't mean you can't make time for rest and relaxation, but do it purposefully – not lazily. (See more on this in the section on 'Changing your life' later in this chapter.)

- **Porn protection** – if you haven't already done so, make sure you have porn protection software on all of your internet devices and also your TV. It's impossible to keep up to date with the latest advances, and even if I could, they'd probably be out of date by the time this book goes to press! But do check out 'Covenant Eyes' and also resources available on Naked Truth's website: (www.nakedtruthproject.com). In addition, contact your ISP and phone provider and ask for parental controls to be put on at source and you should also install accountability software which will send an account of your internet viewing to your accountability partners. The latter will help to deter you from trying to get round any blockers!

MANAGE UNAVOIDABLE TRIGGERS

Unfortunately some triggers are unavoidable. For many people, seeing a sexual image on the street or in the media, or being flirted with by an attractive person or being confronted with an unexpected opportunity such as an unprotected PC can be difficult times to negotiate. For those with an attachment induced addiction, problems within relationships such as conflict or rejection may be triggering and those with a trauma induced addiction may find times of stress or anxiety particularly challenging.

Now I don't know about you, but I've always found this verse in the Bible a little tough:

> *"Blessed is the one who perseveres under trial because, having stood the test, that person will receive the crown of life that the Lord has promised to those who love him."*
> **(JAMES 1:12 NASB)**

And even more difficult,

> *"Dear brothers and sisters, when troubles of any kind come your way, consider it an opportunity for great joy. For you know that when your faith is tested, your endurance has a chance to grow. So let it grow, for when your endurance is fully developed, you will be perfect and complete, needing nothing."*
> **(JAMES 1: 2-4 NLT)**

As we explored earlier in the book, temptations, (aka triggers) are a part of living in a fallen world, but if you're in recovery it's very difficult to feel 'blessed' by them, let alone experience 'great joy,' isn't it?!

But it is undoubtedly true that as you conquer your triggers your confidence in recovery will grow. And when you recognise that these temptations are coming from the devil, not from you, you will develop greater resilience against them. You will also build yourself up as a stronger character and feel closer to God in your everyday life. But the promise of endurance under trial goes beyond the benefits in this world.

1 Peter 1:6-7 (NLT) says,

> *"So be truly glad. There is wonderful joy ahead, even though you have to endure many trials for a little while. These trials will show that your faith is genuine. It is being tested as fire tests and purifies gold—though your faith is far more precious than mere gold. So when your faith remains strong through many trials, it will bring you much praise and glory and honour on the day when Jesus Christ is revealed to the whole world."*

And then later in 1 Peter, this promise is made:

> *"And the God of all grace, who called you to his eternal glory in Christ, after you have suffered a little while,*

> *will himself restore you and make you strong, firm and steadfast."*
> **(1 PETER 5:10)**

So you could summarise the Bible's teaching on temptation that as long as we hang on in there and don't submit, we will be rewarded both in this life, and the next. But our God is one of grace and compassion, He doesn't expect you to just 'hang on in there'! He offers so much more!

In 1 Corinthians 10:13 (ESV) Paul says -

> *"No temptation has overtaken you that is not common to man. God is faithful, and he will not let you be tempted beyond your ability, but with the temptation he will also provide the way of escape, that you may be able to endure it."*

We're going to explore one of those escape routes now.

LEARN TO R.U.N.

The R.U.N. acrostic is one that I developed some years ago and I just can't find the words to express how delighted I am at how successful this relapse prevention strategy is. (I know, I'm a writer, I shouldn't struggle with words!) This acrostic really is a gift from God and it comes from the story of Joseph when he was being tempted by Potiphar's wife. Genesis 39 tells the story of how his master's wife was attracted to him and continually tried to get Joseph into bed.

> *"She kept putting pressure on Joseph day after day, but he refused to sleep with her, and he kept out of her way as much as possible. One day, however, no one else was around when he went in to do his work. She came and grabbed him by his cloak, demanding, "Come on, sleep with me!" Joseph tore himself away, but he left his cloak in her hand as he ran from the house."*
> **(GENESIS 39:9-12 NLT)**

Joseph was doing his best to avoid the temptation, but when it became unavoidable, he ran. Why? Because he knew the consequences if he did and he knew that talking his way out of it wasn't working. And that's precisely what you need to do.

Whatever the trigger or temptation may be, literally get away from the situation – fast. That might mean leaving the house, the office, the hotel, the restaurant, the tube or even the church - whatever it is - get away from the opportunity immediately. And if you can't physically get away, turn away. This is particularly important if you're prone to objectifying and lusting after attractive people. If you can't get away from them, then remember the 3 second rule – count 1, 2 then look away. You can't stop yourself noticing that someone is attractive, but you can obey the 3 second rule and turn away. In addition, use the R.U.N. acrostic to remember:-

- **R**emove yourself immediately from the situation.
- **U**ndistort your thinking – whatever is going round your head telling you that you want to act out is from the devil. Remember James 4:7 (NIV) says, "Resist the devil and he will flee from you".
- **N**ever forget what you have to lose – you made the decision to stop being a sex addict because it was ruining your life - that fact has not changed.

Learning to RUN is the single most important relapse prevention technique there is. I have heard countless stories of relapse when this simple principle had been unheeded. If a trigger is ignored, minimised, flirted with or indulged, it will get bigger and bigger and become stronger and stronger. Imagine a snowball rolling down a mountain. Ignore it, and it will become an avalanche; an avalanche that will engulf you.

There are extra principles you can add to this strategy to maximise your chances of escape. Whilst RUNning, have some techniques ready to distract you from your craving and, if possible, also ones that will get you emotionally and psychologically into a safer space. Below is a list of ideas:-

- **Podcasts** – download and have ready some inspirational speakers. That could be preachers, mentors, TED talks – anything that will get your interest.

- **Music playlist** – ideally tunes that you can sing along to. You can't sing the words to something and easily think about something else. There are suggestions for Christian songs in Chapter 7.

- **Audio book** – something you've been wanting to read for ages or you're already in to.

- **Reading material** – could be Scripture or a Christian book, or a self help book (like this!) or a trashy novel. It really doesn't matter as long as it will distract you.

- **Positive self talk** – think back to the cognitive distortions you read earlier in Chapter 5 and rewrite them as positives. For example, if you're thinking 'It's not that bad', or 'I'm too weak to resist', counteract this with 'It's a sin and all sin is equal to God' and 'I can do anything with God who gives me strength'. There's a list of Bible quotes in chapter 7, so make a note of the ones you feel will help you, along with any others.

- **Photos and mementos** - put together a box of items that give meaning to your life. That could be photos of loved ones, letters, gifts, rewards you've received or words of encouragement from others.

- **Games** – if you're into Tetris or 'Candy Crush' or brain training games, have some downloaded ready for when you need them. Or make sure you have a compendium of crosswords or Sudoku puzzles at the ready.

- **Phone list** – make sure you have a list of contacts to hand. That could be your accountability partners to turn to for prayer, or someone within a recovery group, or a friend who can temporarily distract you.

Whatever you choose to do while you're RUNning, do it for at least 20 minutes. There's only a bit of under-researched science to back the idea that 20 minutes distraction is important, but much, much more anecdotal evidence from clients. The thing to remember is that whatever you choose, make sure it's accessible for whatever situation you may find yourself in and keep doing it until the temptation subsides.

Before we end this section on managing unavoidable triggers, we need to look at what is perhaps the most common trigger, but also one of the most misunderstood; how to handle sexual urges.

SEXUAL URGES

One of the most challenging triggers for many addicts is their sex drive, especially during the early days of recovery and if they've chosen to undertake a period of abstinence. Although acting out is about dopamine arousal in the brain, rather than testosterone desire in the groin, there's no doubt that feeling sexually aroused can be a significant aggravating factor to managing triggers. In Chapter 1 we talked about positive sexuality and I hope from that you have made a decision about what's right for you. If you haven't, you need to make a commitment to what's OK and what's not OK, now. Without firm boundaries, you will be leaving the door open to slips and relapses.

The area that most Christians struggle with, especially in early recovery, is whether or not masturbation is OK. As we discussed in Chapter 1, as long as this is done mindfully, without lust, then it may fit with your Christian values, but if it doesn't, then it is of course not OK for you. But if you're in a relationship, you may choose to share all sexual behaviours within your relationship. Either way, many people in early recovery find a period of complete abstinence helpful.

Committing to a period of abstinence provides many benefits. If you're married, it is an opportunity to demonstrate your recovery to your partner and develop other ways of being intimate with each other. In addition, for both married and single people, abstinence provides space to discover what your innate sex drive is really like. Many people with sex and porn addiction have completely lost touch with their own libido. Like someone who constantly over eats, they have forgotten what hunger feels like. And like hunger, it allows the opportunity to experience the fact that urges and cravings ebb and flow. If you've ever fasted you'll know that hunger pangs are uncomfortable, but they are not constant and they are bearable. Similarly, during sexual abstinence you will almost certainly experience sexual desire, but if you distract yourself with some kind of physical diversion, such as exercise, a walk, laughing with friends, or even taking a cold shower, the sensations will pass. The most important thing to do is not to dwell on the physical urge, or allow your mind to entertain thoughts of satiation, but rather to immediately do something that will distract your body and your mind. Over time you will learn to live with the temporary discomfort and gain a greater sense of control over your sexual impulses – thereby strengthening your confidence in long term recovery.

The length and extent of abstinence depends on your

individual circumstances, for example, the situation for a 20-year-old single person may be very different from a 50 year old in a committed sexual relationship, but most choose a period between 30 and 90 days. My suggestion would be to start with 30 days, and if that's comfortable, continue longer. And even if you do have a 'slip' during that time, don't be disheartened and go back to day 1. But rather learn from that slip and recommit. If you manage 90 days with just a couple of slips, that's a great start to your recovery. There are lots of resources in the next chapter that you can schedule into your diary and use while you work through your abstinence period.

Changing your life

The ultimate goal of addiction recovery is to develop a lifestyle that no longer needs the compulsive behaviour. That doesn't mean there won't continue to be occasions when you 'want' to act out, but they will be few and far between and you will no longer 'need' to. In this section we're going to look at some of the practical things you can do to change your life and we're also going to look at the spiritual truths that can help you to break the chains of addiction forever.

SPIRITUAL CHANGE

Earlier in the book we were looking at how grace and faith are the antidote to denial, and those two mainstays of Christianity, are also the antidote to addiction. Why do we humans find it so hard to let go of sinful behaviours? Yes, living in a fallen world alongside the devil is one reason, but the other is that we struggle to truly believe that God loves us unconditionally and wants what's best for us. We fear we're too broken, beyond redemption and that God is not enough to satisfy us. But as we explored in the preface of this book, in reality, we almost always settle for so much less than God desires for us.

C.S Lewis said

> *"It would seem that Our Lord finds our desires not too strong, but too weak. We are half-hearted creatures, fooling about with drink and sex and ambition when infinite joy is offered us, like an ignorant child who wants to go on making mud pies in a slum because he cannot imagine what is meant by the offer of a holiday at the sea. We are far too easily pleased."*
> **(THE WEIGHT OF GLORY, 1941)**

The bottom line is this – getting into recovery means getting right with God. It means 'living' the first and most important commandment.

> *"Love the Lord your God with all your heart and with all your soul and with all your mind and with all your strength."*
> **(MATTHEW 12: 31 NIV)**

This command is perhaps impossible this side of heaven, but with grace and faith in His infinite love for us, we can get closer each day.

You do not have to see this as a sacrifice or as something you're 'giving up', you can see this as something you've grown out of as part of your spiritual growth and maturity. When the Israelites were getting frustrated that their sacrifices to God seemed to be falling on deaf ears, the profit Micah answered

> *"...what does the LORD require of you? To act justly and to love mercy and to walk humbly with your God."*
> **(MICAH 6:8 NIV)**

In other words, your actions should be honorable, your heart should be loving and compassionate and your daily life should be alongside your Father, knowing and trusting that He is in control and knows what's best, not you.

Getting into recovery is a great opportunity for getting closer to God; developing new spiritual practices or reviving old ones. If you want to explore this more, there are some great books listed in the next chapter to inspire and guide you. So for now, let's look at some of the practical stuff.

PHYSICAL CHANGE

It's often said that a healthy mind starts with a healthy body, and there is undoubtedly some truth in that. We are not always fit and healthy, but we can do everything within our power to make the most of the physical frame that God has put our soul into.

> *"Do you not know that your bodies are temples of the Holy Spirit, who is in you, whom you have received from God? You are not your own; you were bought at a price. Therefore honour God with your bodies."*
> **(1 CORINTHIANS 6:19-20 NIV)**

In plain English, that means look after yourself! Eat healthily, exercise frequently, develop a regular sleeping routine and take time to relax.

A lot of Christians have a problem

with relaxing and then wonder why they struggle with burn out and start resenting the service they offer others. But we are commanded to love others 'as we love ourselves' and even God took a day off from creation to chill out and marvel at his work! The principle of the Sabbath day of rest is well documented for spiritual, physical and emotional health, so make sure you take it. Furthermore, we know that healthy bodies find it easier to manage triggers and cope with unexpected stress. And the neural pathways in your brain that have developed the addiction will regenerate faster.

EMOTIONAL CHANGE

As we've explored throughout this book, addictive behaviours become a way of managing difficult emotions. In earlier chapters, you were invited to explore what some of those issues were for you. I know I said it then, but I'm going to stress it again – if you do not do the work to develop healthier ways of managing difficult emotions, you will always be at risk of relapse. Find people you can trust and talk to. Read self help books. See a counsellor or pastoral care giver. Emotional pain is inevitable in this world, but struggling with it alone is a choice you don't have to make. I have always loved the story in Mark 2 where the four friends ripped a roof off a house to get the paralysed man to Jesus – now that's friendship! And somewhere, that support is there for you too. But God doesn't just send others to help us with our pain, He is alongside us in it too.

> *"You keep track of all my sorrows. You have collected all my tears in your bottle. You have recorded each one in your book."*
> **(PSALM 56:8 NLT)**

Before we end this chapter, there's one final area to consider – and that's how you can move from 'Finding Freedom' to 'Walking in Freedom'.

WALKING IN FREEDOM

Apparently the great evangelist Billy Graham shocked his audience one day when he announced that there was something he could do, that God couldn't. The audience, no doubt frowning and waiting impatiently, then heard him say, "I can remember my sins". The Bible talks in many places of how God 'forgets' our sins. Of course, He doesn't forget in the human way that we forget things, but once repented, he removes them and chooses not to look at them again. Psalm 103 says:

> *"As far as the east is from the west, so far has he removed our transgressions from us."*
> **(PSALM 103:12 NIV)**

Now human memory is a great gift, and remembering our sins and the pain we've caused others can support recovery. But if you dwell on the past and find yourself continuing to live with self retribution and shame, then you are not living in the redeemed freedom promised you by Christ's death on the cross. If your behaviours have hurt others, then you need to show appropriate remorse and reparation, but if you're ever to move forward in recovery, at some stage you will need to follow Christ's example and forgive yourself. God promises us redemption and restoration from our sin.

> *"For I will take you out of the nations; I will gather you from all the countries and bring you back into your own land. I will sprinkle clean water on you, and you will be clean; I will cleanse you from all your impurities and from all your idols. I will give you a new heart and put a new spirit in you; I will remove from you your heart of stone and give you a heart of flesh. And I will put my Spirit in you and move you to follow my decrees and be careful to keep my laws."*
> **(EZEKIEL 36: 24-27 NIV)**

There's another reason why you should choose not to remember your past. Jesus summarised this in three words in Luke 17 when He was teaching about the coming of the Kingdom of God. He said, "Remember Lot's wife?"

In Genesis 19 the story is told that when Lot and his family were being rescued by the angels from the coming destruction of Sodom, they were given the instruction "Do not look behind" but Lot's wife did, and she was turned to a pillar of salt. We're not told exactly why she did this, but we can surmise that she did not really want to leave. But the lesson here is that if you're tempted to look back at your old ways with longing, remember that it never gave you comfort then, and it won't now. Like Lot's family, you have been saved from destruction and your life is ahead of you, not behind.

Like the Prodigal Son, the journey home may be a long one, but the cloak, the ring, the sandals and the fatted calf are waiting for you and for those you love and care for. Indeed, they've always been there waiting for us all (See Luke 15:11-32).

I want to end this part of the book with some wonderfully wise words from John Newton:

> *I am not what I ought to be,*
> *nor what I wish to be,*
> *or what I hope to be,*
> *but by the grace of God,*
> *I am not what I once was.*

Reflection

In this chapter we have looked at the three pillars of recovery:

- Accountability – the importance of sharing your recovery journey with others. Not only will this break through the secrecy and shame that fuels addiction, but it will also provide essential support and challenge.
- Relapse prevention – recognising your triggers and avoiding them if you possibly can and having a list of techniques and strategies you will use when you find yourself needing to RUN from the inevitable unavoidable triggers that you will face.
- Changing your life – true recovery means developing a lifestyle that no longer needs your addiction. That requires spiritual, physical and emotional change.

It's important to start thinking about how your life will be different once you're walking in an addiction free life. Creating visual reminders is a powerful tool to inspire and encourage you when things feel impossible.

In this space, write down specific artists or creative ideas that you can collect for inspiration and a reminder of that different life. For example: a beautiful photo of your family, a memoir of when you achieved a goal or a painting that speaks of God's love. Spend some time reflecting on Charlie Mackesy's Prodigal Son/Daughter to start you off.

Reflection Notes

> "I am not defined by the appetites I resist but by the virtues I embrace."
> — KRIS VALLOTTON

CHAPTER SIX

Porn widows & widowers

Pornography hurts not just those who view it, but also the partners of those who use it – in many different ways. A partner's self esteem can be damaged as they suddenly feel compared to beautiful young bodies with alluring exaggerated proportions, rarely achievable without surgery. They can feel in competition with bodies that perform the sexual act with apparent passion and vigour - bodies whose sole purpose is to excite and entice. However, it is no longer true that porn only portrays conventionally beautiful bodies. 'Couple next door' genres grow in popularity. It is possible to easily access pornographic images of all body types - whether large, small, tall, short, young, old, white, black, blonde, brunette – people can find it all online. Nonetheless, what no partner can compete with, is the infinite variety that porn provides nor the athletic enthusiasm with which the porn star performs.

When you find yourself in a relationship with someone who watches porn, whether that's recreational or compulsive viewing, it can create profound feelings of betrayal and insecurity. Many partners feel desperately hurt that what should have been a private and intimate act, discovered together through the bond of their love and marriage, has already been explored elsewhere. For some that may have been in previous relationships, but for others it's been onscreen. Some spouses discover that their partner's only sex education has come from viewing porn and hence they find their relationship burdened with unrealistic expectations.

When partners continue to watch porn, often secretly until they're discovered, their spouses feel abandoned, rejected and deceived. Whilst physical adultery may not have taken place, porn-viewing is undoubtedly a breach of trust and fidelity. As one woman painfully shared with me, "he chooses to have sex with women onscreen, rather than make love to me." And of course there are those whose partner's porn viewing has escalated through addiction from voyeuristic to interactive online sex chat, webcam sex, visiting sex workers or meeting people for sex through hook up or dating sites.

If your spouse is watching porn then the first thing to do is to talk about it. Share how you feel and how it impacts you. If you have difficulties in your relationship, commit to working through them together. If your partner is also a Christian, commit to pray together and seek counsel from other trusted believers if you can. If your partner isn't a Christian, then you can still turn to God in prayer and others for support. Remember, the Bible says,

> *"Do not be afraid, for you will not be put to shame; and do not feel humiliated, for you will not be disgraced... For your husband is your Maker, whose name is the Lord of hosts, and your redeemer is the Holy One who is called the God of all the earth."*
> **(ISAIAH 54:4-5 NASV)**

If your partner is unable to quit porn, or if you already know it has become an addiction, there is more help in the coming chapters - as well as more support for you in the next section.

Support for partners

Discovering your partner or spouse is addicted to porn or sex is devastating. And the shame for partners, especially Christian partners can be crippling. Not only is it a betrayal of them, but of their shared faith in God. For partners of those in Christian service or ministry, the sense of hypocrisy drives the shame even deeper in their heart and lives. No one expects to be in a relationship with an addict and because, unlike any other addiction, sex addiction has no physical side effects, most partners are completely stunned by the discovery or disclosure. "He's not that type!" is a common refrain for partners to make, a statement that not only conveys the common misunderstandings of sex and porn addiction, but also the shock and disbelief that so many partners feel.

When partners first find out that they've been betrayed, whether that's by a porn addiction or offline physical infidelity, they are initially plagued by questions such as:

Why did they do this?
What's wrong with me?
Who is this stranger I thought was my spouse?
Has my whole marriage been a lie?
Can I ever trust them again?
Should I leave my relationship?
Who can I talk to?
What should I do?
Where is God?

These are common and understandable questions, and in time and with patience and courage, you will find more answers. But like all Christians in times of crisis, we grow when we trust God, in spite of our unanswered questions. Proverbs 3:5-6 (NIV) says,

> *"Trust in the Lord with all your heart and lean not on your own understanding, acknowledge him in all your ways and he will direct your paths."*

Unfortunately there is not enough space in this book to share with you everything I know from my experience of working with hundreds of partners of sex and porn addicts, but I will give you the essentials. You may find it useful to get a copy of my book, 'Sex Addiction – The Partners Perspective' (Routledge, 2015) which is dedicated to helping partners survive the betrayal and pain of sex and porn addiction. Many well-meaning partners make the mistake of throwing themselves into supporting their partner's recovery, rather than focusing on their own needs. And regrettably, in the long term, this can actually make the addiction harder to overcome and delay healing both your wounds and the relationship.

Understanding 'The Three C's'

There's a mantra that we use in our partner-support programmes that I have shamelessly stolen from "Al Anon" – the support groups for partners of alcoholics. It's known as the 'Three C's' and they are:

>You didn't *Cause* it
>You can't *Control* it
>You can't *Cure* it

We will look at each of these in turn and hopefully you'll agree that you need to make this your mantra too.

YOU DIDN'T *CAUSE* IT

As you'll see if you read on in the book, sex and porn

addiction often has its root in early childhood experiences. In fact, most people who develop porn addiction say they started using porn before they were 16 – often earlier. It's a condition that develops slowly over time so most likely, your partner was already addicted, or well on the road to addiction before you'd even met. Many people with sex or porn addiction, and their partners, assume that a healthy, satisfying sex life will be sufficient to help them stop. But that's like assuming that if a compulsive overeater gets their 5-a-day, they'll no longer want more food.

As you'll also see as you read on, sex addiction has nothing to do with sex at all, but is a coping strategy that has gone awry. Nothing you did – absolutely nothing – caused your partner's addiction. Perhaps you had relationship problems or you know that your sex life wasn't what your spouse had hoped for, but that doesn't make someone addicted. They may have turned to their addiction as a way of avoiding dealing with relationship difficulties, but those difficulties didn't cause it. Your partner must take full responsibility for the choices they make to act out, rather than address any problems they may have had in their lives. It is their choices that caused the addiction to take root and escalate, not yours. So let me say it again – nothing you did – absolutely nothing – caused your partner's addiction.

YOU CAN'T *CONTROL* IT

In the same way as you are not responsible for causing your spouse's addiction, you are also not responsible for controlling it. Indeed, trying to do so may not only impede your partner's recovery, but also damage your relationship. Your partner has to take complete responsibility for what caused their addiction and for controlling it. As we'll discuss later in this chapter where we talk about rebuilding trust, it's important that you put accountability strategies in place to protect yourself, such as installing porn blockers on internet devices and sharing diaries and agreeing other guidelines. But those principles are there for you, not to control your partner. Their recovery is their job. If you put yourself in a position where you are monitoring and policing your partner's behaviour, that will damage the equality of the relationship. Rather than being the equal partner that God intended, you will be playing the role of parent. And in the long term, parent and child marriages, rather than husband and wife, are never happy ones. You can't, nor should you try, to control your partner.

YOU CAN'T *CURE* IT

Your partner's recovery is their responsibility and as much as you might want to be supportive in their journey of redemption, you can't do it for them. The desire to cure often comes from a place of fear and insecurity, wanting to feel that you have the power to make everything alright again. But if you accept the fact that you didn't cause the addiction, how can you possibly believe that you can cure it? Ultimately, God is the healer and your partner's recovery is between them and God. The other problem with trying to cure your partner's addiction is that it robs you of the energy and self-compassion that you need to start your own recovery from betrayal. Your time is better spent focusing on yourself, not them.

Countless people have started to put their lives back together based on these foundations. Hopefully you now understand the Three C's and will begin to believe in them and practise them for yourself. Knowing and operating from these principles can lead you to a place of being able to start to heal. So, now it's time to help you, look after you.

Learning to S.U.R.F.

Many partners describe the seemingly endless painful emotions that accompany the discovery of sex or porn addiction like being lost at sea in a storm. There's no land in sight, no anchor and all you can do is bob up and down, hoping and praying that you won't drown in the pain. There's a saying I particularly like, "You can't stop the waves, but you can learn to surf" – so what follows are some surfing instructions.

S – Survive the trauma
U – Understand the cycle of reaction
R – Repair your self worth
F – Face the future

Let's look at each in more depth.

SURVIVE THE TRAUMA OF DISCOVERY

However you discover your partner's addiction, whether that's through endless detective work, sudden disclosure, or the more common agonising gradual realisation process, shock is most likely the first emotion you'll experience. Even if you had suspicions for a while, when reality hits, shock follows. As the numbness of shock begins to fade, many partners experience a flood of emotions that can feel totally overwhelming. Anger, fear, grief, despair, shame and disgust are commonplace. It's also normal to desperately seek comfort from your partner – the person you've most likely relied on in times of trouble. Simultaneously you may also want to hurt them, shut them out and never want to see them again.

The emotional roller coaster usually runs for at least six months, during which time, your energies will be spent in just trying to hold on. During the early weeks and months, many partners find themselves having to endure numerous painful confessions or discoveries. Having picked themselves up from the last disclosure or discovery, and believing when they were told they now knew everything, they get knocked down again as more and more of the truth leaks out.

It's hard to describe the emotional pain that so many partners experience. Well-meaning friends and untrained counsellors may try to offer comfort and support, but discovering addiction is not the same as any other kind of infidelity. As the addiction nearly always pre-dates the relationship and full recovery may take a lifetime, it can feel as though there is no 'before' to get back to, or 'after' to look forward to. Many partners are wracked with self-doubt and fear. They no longer trust their partner or themselves. Many doubt their ability to know the difference between fiction and reality and to trust their own instincts and feelings. The shock, fear and anger is not just at what their partner has done, but at themselves for not knowing what was going on right in front of them.

It's essential in the early weeks and months after discovery to get support from others and to have people to talk to who understand your experience. Get prayer support, lean on your Father and be kind to yourself. Don't be tempted to make any important decisions about your future during this time of emotional instability. If you need a break from your partner, then do so. But don't make any permanent changes until you are confident that your feet are back on solid ground again.

UNDERSTAND THE CYCLE OF REACTION

Once the initial shock of discovery has passed, many partners also find themselves trapped in a cycle. One minute they feel as though they can cope and they are beginning to make sense of what's happened and get themselves back together again – then BANG! – they're back to square one again. The image below illustrates the 'cycle of reaction' that so many partners get trapped in – a repeating pattern of what often feels like an out-of-control reaction to the trauma of sex addiction. We'll look at each stage now.

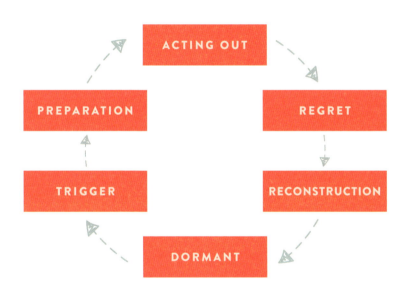

Dormant - This phase of the cycle is where you feel reasonably OK and on top of things. But it's the place where our history lives – the experiences of childhood and previous relationships that made you into the person you are today. These experiences are influencing the way you are reacting and responding to this crisis. Identifying your issues can help you to ensure that you're not unconsciously replaying old scripts, but responding positively and appropriately in the here and now.

Trigger – There are many things that can trigger a partner, often without warning. It could be a harmless comment by a friend, an attractive woman on the street, a storyline in a TV show or film. Or passing a road sign to a place where you know your partner previously acted out, or a church sermon on the importance of fidelity in relationships. Or perhaps your partner checking their phone or closing down the computer when you walk into the room. Some partners describe themselves as feeling constantly on tenterhooks – not knowing when they'll be ambushed again and thrown back into the maelstrom of emotion.

Preparation – During the preparation phase of the cycle, thoughts and feelings run amok as you ruminate on the trigger. Some partners find themselves suddenly thrown into suspicion and insecurity and start surreptitiously seeking further evidence of betrayal. Or they allow painful old memories to come back to the forefront of their mind and relive them. As the thoughts and feelings build and build, it's just a matter of time before they explode into a reactive emotion or behaviour.

Reactive behaviours – Of course it's understandable to have powerful emotions after discovering addiction, but partners need to feel confident that they are able to choose how they respond to, and express those emotions, rather than reacting to them. When feelings of anger explode into rage or revenge, or sadness is expressed through overeating, binge drinking, or withdrawal from social situations, then the impact damages you. Similarly, if you find yourself having panic attacks or sinking into depression, then this is not a healthy response for you. Feelings are natural and often out of our conscious control when triggered, but what you do with them can become your choice.

Regret – Many partners feel enormous regret about how they behave during an emotional outburst. I remember one partner who had always believed herself to be a calm and peaceful women saying, "I've become a stranger to myself!" when her anger boiled over into bitter and cruel recriminations. The regret may not necessarily be towards how you've treated your partner, but how you've treated yourself. You may also have shame about how out of control you felt. Many Christian women find themselves reacting in ways that are not in line with their beliefs. These unfamiliar behaviours leave them feeling further from God and their fellow Christians.

Reconstruction – During this phase, you will be putting yourself back together again. That might mean making apologies to others, confessing your sins to God, praying for greater emotional control and promising to be stronger in the future. But unless you've spent time understanding what's happening in your dormant phase and why you react the way you do, then the next trigger may result in history repeating itself and further shame and self-blame and damage to you and those you care about.

The goal of recovery for partners is to end the cycle of reaction and confidently replace it with an ability to choose appropriate responses instead of feeling overwhelmed by destructive emotional reactions. It takes time and effort to do this, but it's something that all partners must do in order to regain a sense of safety and stability. There's much more advice on how to do this, as well as how to recognise and manage triggers in a healthy way in my book, 'Sex Addiction – The Partner's Perspective.'

REPAIR SELF-WORTH

Perhaps the most damaging impact of sex and pornography addiction is what it does to a partner's self esteem. Even if you have succeeded in rationally believing the Three C's, it can take much longer for the truth of that to reach you emotionally and sink into your heart. Many partners wrestle with self-doubt for years after discovering addiction. While they tell themselves, "It wasn't my fault and it wasn't about me", they check their hair a dozen times before leaving the house and invest in new make up and clothes to boost their confidence. Many fear what others will think of them if they stay in the relationship. Christian women in particular may feel that divorce is not an option for them and wonder if their Christian sisters pity them.

There are many good Christian books on improving self-esteem some of which are listed in Chapter 7, but for now, all I can say is that whatever you've been through and whatever your spouse has done to you, you are as valuable and special to God as you ever were. Indeed, God promises to be especially close in our time of need. Psalm 34:18 (NLT) says, "The Lord is close to the broken hearted, He rescues those whose spirits are crushed." It is so hard to believe that God is still in control when our world is falling apart, but know that it's true, even when you can't feel it.

FACE THE FUTURE

Have you ever wondered what God's plan is for your life? Most Christians do. Have you wondered if your pain right now was part of it? No. God never intended his people to suffer, but because of The Fall and His loving gift of free will, we do suffer. You are the victim of sin, but God can and will work through this experience in your life. Romans 8:28 (NIV) confidently tells us,

> *"And we know that in all things, God works for the good of those who love him." Whatever the future holds, your life is not over and you are not alone.*

After the discovery of porn all partners find themselves facing a different future to the one they thought. Until you know what that looks like, you will almost certainly benefit from spending time focusing on the aspects of your life that give you meaning and purpose, outside of your marriage. That might be your career, children, friendships, fellowship, Christian service, recreational pursuits or any number of other things. You are much more than just the partner of an addict. You're a creation of God, made for His purpose. That purpose has not gone.

For some, the future may mean separation from their partner, whether that's your decision or theirs. Whilst we know that God does not desire divorce, neither does He desire pain. And if separation or divorce is the path that you choose to take, you can be assured that God's love for you does not depend on your status - as married, or divorced. It is, of course, not a decision to be taken lightly or quickly, nor without much prayer and spiritual direction. If your relationship is going to survive addiction, you need to be staying in it out of love, not duty. And whatever you do, at some stage you will need to forgive.

Forgiveness is essential for spouses recovering from their partner's addiction. We know that the Bible commands that we forgive and tells us it is not just out of compassion for others, but also for ourselves. Forgiveness is psychologically essential for our mental health and one of the most powerful tools for healing the human heart. It's not easy or quick – forgiveness is a process, not a one-off event. It is a gradual release of the feelings that keep us bound to our pain. Some partners harbour the misconception that not forgiving will somehow protect them from future pain or the risk of their partner relapsing – but that is not the case. Forgiveness gives you freedom and opens the way for God's grace to heal you and your relationship.

As your SURFing skills improve, you will find the waves of emotion more tolerable and, assuming your partner is remorseful and in recovery, you'll hopefully have some energy left to consider how to rebuild trust.

REBUILDING TRUST

No relationship can survive without trust, but there is no fast track to trusting someone who may have so brutally betrayed you. There's much more on rebuilding trust in my partner's book, but here we'll look at the essentials.

Honesty

For trust to be rebuilt, both of you need to commit to complete and total honesty. Honesty about your feelings, thoughts and behaviours. For most partners, rebuilding trust starts with complete honesty about the 'acting out' behaviours that happened in the past. Until this is done, many partners find themselves still grappling with doubts and suspicions. The person with the addiction has potentially left a door open to continue acting out. However, it is not helpful for partners to know the intricate details of pornography viewing behaviours. Rather than providing security, they are much more likely to build painful visual images that get in the way of healing. If you're unsure how much you want or need to know or if you're not sure you're strong enough yet to hear any further disclosures, then speak to someone trained in this field who can guide and help you through the process.

When talking about honesty, it's important to remember that this needs to be sensitive and respectful of others. Many people in recovery will join support groups where they will be expected to maintain the group's confidentiality. Furthermore, complete honesty about every time an addict feels triggered can be insensitive and cause more pain, rather than healing. Remember that the opposite of honesty is not necessarily dishonesty. It is the motivation behind our choice to share or not share that makes the difference. If information would be harmful to someone, then it may be best not to say it, but if you're choosing to remain silent simply to protect yourself, then you need to think again. The next section should help you consider this further.

Accountability

Building accountability into your relationship can be one of the quickest ways of rebuilding trust and helping you as a partner to feel more secure. I often suggest that partners write an accountability contract. This is something that is done together and collaboratively, and provides an opportunity to consider ways in which both can be helped to avoid triggers. For example, a partner may hold the passwords on internet devices and porn protection and accountability software. You might agree to using Facetime to communicate with each other so you know where you are when apart, and begin to use the 'track my phone' settings on your smart phone. Some couples agree to boundaries around their television viewing and computer usage and agree that they will begin to go to bed at the same time. The type of contract you create will depend on the type of acting out behaviour, but the goal is to do this together and create something that will benefit you both. The more accountable your partner can be, the fewer doubts you will feel.

Empathy

This may seem like an odd thing to be saying in a section on rebuilding trust, but if your partner can't understand and demonstrate that they know how you feel, it's difficult to believe that they won't hurt you again. In my recovery groups, I always tell addicts that it's not enough to sit silently and remorsefully feeling their partner's pain; they need to show that they understand it. Many people with addiction become defensive when challenged, particularly when they've done nothing wrong. But, by demonstrating that they understand their partner's triggers and recognise that it will take time to overcome the pain, they can begin to offer the reassurance that partners desperately need.

It's also important to be able to share that you understand how each is struggling and show gratitude at the changes that are being made. Recovery is hard work for both of you and you need all the encouragement you can get.

Honesty, accountability and empathy are the building blocks of trust, but remember your partner will never be able to prove that they have 'not' done something. Ultimately the only way that trust will be rebuilt is by understanding what caused and maintained your partner's addiction and seeing that those issues have been fully resolved and worked through. As you'll see later in the book the first rule of recovery is 'change your life'. When you can see that your partner has changed not just their physical habits, but their emotional and spiritual life too, then your trust will grow. Overcoming sex and pornography addiction is not a one off event, but a lifetime commitment. Many partners struggle with the idea that they will be living with someone who is in recovery, someone who may be susceptible to relapse for the rest of their life. The risk of relapse is always there, though it's certainly not inevitable. If the addiction was relatively mild, then your partner may struggle with little more than an occasional sinful thought, but if it was severe then your future may include significant lifestyle changes and challenges.

As Christians, we are called to put our trust in God, not in man. So if you trust that God is looking after you and your marriage, you can know that whatever happens, He will not forsake you.

> *"For I alone know the plans I have for you, plans to bring you prosperity, not disaster, plans to bring about the future you hope for."*
> **(JEREMIAH 29:11 GNT).**

Let me end this chapter with a story of hope.

Real lives

Sophie and John had been married for 9 years when she discovered his internet porn use. At first, she assumed he had turned to porn during a difficult pregnancy with their second child that had affected their sex life, and when she confronted him, he assured her it was infrequent and he would stop. But some of his story didn't add up so she secretly trawled through his browsing history, and was shocked by, not only the extent of his viewing, but the material he was looking at. When she confronted him again, he confessed that he knew it was a problem and he didn't understand why he looked at some of the things he did, and again promised that it was in the past. Over the next few months, she trusted him, but over time he reverted to staying up late at night using the computer. When she tried to look at his viewing history again, she discovered that he'd deleted it. Sophie found herself becoming increasingly secretive and sneaky, and whilst she knew she would be betraying John, she asked her brother who was an IT expert for help. She lied to John saying the computer was broken and 2 days later confronted him with the additional information her brother had found. Not only had John been looking at porn for over 5 years, but it was often for hours and hours at a time, and he had also been chatting to women online and had a secret email account through which he corresponded with some of them. Sophie was devastated and exploded with rage at John. For the next few weeks she alternated between vengeful outbursts and floods of tears.

Sophie and John came for help. John joined a Christian recovery programme and Sophie came to a partner's support group. They also sought prayer support from their church. John made a full disclosure to Sophie which included that he had also met 3 women for sex. Although the pain initially felt unbearable, Sophie developed strategies to cope and a support network to carry her through. John was able to explain that at the root of his addiction was a history of low self esteem and fears that Sophie was 'too good for him'. Sophie shared insecurities with John and explained that her rage at him stemmed from a fear of being trapped in a bad marriage like her mother had been. Over the following year they began to rebuild their life together, becoming more open and honest with each other than they had ever been. Whilst neither of them would want to go through the experience again, they're both able to see how God used the experience to show each of them His healing grace. They both agree that they feel closer to each other than ever before, and closer to God too.

Reflection

In this chapter we have explored:

- The devastating impact compulsive pornography use has on partners
- The essential 3 C's for partner recovery – you didn't Cause it, you can't Control it and you can't Cure it
- Strategies for dealing with the shock of finding out your partner is addicted to porn
- How to rebuild trust

Having read this chapter, imagine a scale of 0-10, where 0 equals totally devastated and 10 equals feeling a sense of God's peace about what's happened. Where would you put yourself on that scale?

Now think about what you could do to move just one point up that scale? That might be talking to someone, spending more time in prayer, taking time out to comfort and look after yourself, talking to your partner? Or indeed, all of these things.

If you are the partner of an addict, which of the three C's presents the most challenges to you today?

Put some time aside to contemplate on this Scripture from Isaiah 26:3-4 (NLT).

What is God saying to you through these words?

"You will keep in perfect peace all who trust in you, all whose thoughts are fixed on you! Trust in the Lord always, for the Lord God is the eternal Rock."

For further support and resources for partners and spouses visit www.nakedtruthproject.com

Reflection Notes

CHAPTER SEVEN

Further help, advice
& resources

This chapter is broken into two parts and provides further help and resources, for people with addiction, for partners, for friends, pastoral carers, counsellors and church leaders. The first section provides details of recommended books, websites and support groups. Please note that not all these resources are specifically Christian, though they are all ones that I would recommend. The second section offers suggestions for further spiritual reflection.

Recommended reading and resources

BOOKS

On addiction...

- 'Addiction & Grace', Gerald G. May (Harper Collins, 2007)
- 'Addiction & Virtue', Kent Dunnington (IVP Academic, 2011)
- 'Oh Brave New Church', Mark Stibbe (Longman & Todd, 1995.)

On sex addiction...

- 'A Couples Guide to Sexual Addiction', Paldrom Collins and George Collins (Adams Media, 2011)
- 'Erotic Intelligence', Alexandra Katehakis (HCI, 2010)
- 'Hope After Betrayal-Healing When Sexual Addiction Invades Your Marriage', Meg Wilson (Kregel Publications, 2007)
- 'Out of the Shadows - Understanding Sexual Addiction', Patrick Carnes (Hazelden Publishing, 2001)
- 'Sex Addiction – The Partner's Perspective', Paula Hall (Routledge, 2015)
- 'Understanding & Treating Sex Addiction', Paula Hall (Routledge, 2012)

- *'Your Brain on Porn – Internet Pornography and the Emerging Science of Addiction'*, Gary Wilson (Commonwealth Publishing, 2015)
- *'Your Sexually Addicted Spouse – How Partners Can Cope and Heal'*, Barbara Steffens and Marsha Means (New Horizon Press Publishers Inc, 2009)
- *'Wired for Intimacy – How Pornography Hijacks the Male Brain'*, William Struthers (IVP Books, 2009)

On sex and sexuality...

- *'Sex God – Exploring the Endless Connections Between Sexuality and Spirituality'*, Rob Bell (HarperOne, 2012)
- *'God Loves Sex – An Honest Conversation About Sexual Desire And Holiness* Dan Allender and Temper Longman (Baker Books, 2014)
- *'Dangerous Honesty – Stories of Women Who Have Escaped the Destructive Power of Pornography'*, Karin Cooke (Naked Truth Resources, 2015)
- *The Dating Dilemma'*, Rachel Gardner & Andre Adefope (IVP, 2013)

On emotional health...

- *'Boundaries – When to Say Yes, When to Say No, To Take Control of Your Life'*, Dr Henry Cloud and Dr John Townsend (Zondervan, 2002)
- *'Emotionally Healthy Spirituality'*, Peter Scazzero (Peter Scazzero, 2011)
- *'Finding Hope when Life Goes Wrong'*, Norman Wright (Revell, 2012)
- *'Improving Your Relationship – For Dummies'*, Paula Hall (John Wiley & Sons, 2010)
- *'You Can Change: God's Transforming Power for Our Sinful Behaviour and Negative Emotions'*, Tim Chester (IVP, 2008)

On confidence and emotions...

- *'In security – living a confident life'*, Ems Hancock (River 2015)
- *'Overcoming Sinful Anger: How to Master Your Emotions and Bring Peace to Your Life'*, Fr T Morrow, T G Morrow. (Sophia Institute Press 2015)

On spirituality...

- *'Counterfeit Gods: When the Empty Promises of Love, Money and Power Let You Down'*, Timothy Keller (Hodder & Stoughton, 2010)
- *'Desiring God Meditations of a Christian Hedonist'*, John Piper (Multnomah, 2011)
- *'Not the Way It's Supposed to Be - A Breviary of Sin'*, Cornelius Plantainga (Eerdmans, 1996)
- *'We Become What We Worship - A Biblical Theology of Idolatry'*, G.K. Beale (IVP Academic, 2008)

ONLINE INFORMATION & SUPPORT

www.clicktokick.com

Online recovery groups for people who want to quit porn, facilitated by trained mentors in the field. The groups are provided online and consist of 8 x 1 hour sessions. There is no fixed fee but a donation to the Naked Truth Project is requested.

www.paulahall.co.uk

Information and video resources explaining sex and porn addiction and information on our individual, partner and couple services that can be provided via video conferencing. At www.paulahall.co.uk/form you'll find our free advice message boards which are run by people in recovery as well as our therapists.

www.sexaddictionhelp.co.uk
A free online self-help tool for sex and porn addiction, created by Paula Hall.

www.yourbrainonporn.com
A brilliant resource for any information and research you may want about porn addiction. Not Christian, but always up to date and has some good facts.

www.nakedtruthproject.com
Naked Truth is the flagship initiative of Visible (www.visibleministries.com) and seeks to open eyes and free lives from the damaging impact of pornography through awareness, education and recovery programmes.

COUNSELLING & THERAPY SERVICES

ACC (Association of Christian Counsellors) – www.acc-org.uk
This is the national association of trained Christian counsellors. Please note, not all will have training or experience in addiction, so do check before committing to therapy.

ATSAC – Association for Treatment of Sex Addiction & Compulsivity – www.atsac.co.uk
The UK's professional body for therapists trained in sex and porn addiction. Not all are Christians, so do ask the question if you particularly want to work with someone of faith.

Paula Hall & Associates – www.paulahall.co.uk
This organisation specialises in sex and porn addiction and provides dedicated faith- based services. Centred in Leamington Spa and London, this organisation offer therapy via video conferencing all round the world, as well as intensive recovery groups for addicts and their partners.

12 Step Support Groups

There are three 12-step groups that work specifically with people with sex and porn addiction. These groups, based on the principles of AA, are confidential and peer led. You can get further details about each group and a list of locations where meetings are held at: www.saa-recovery.org.uk (Sex Addicts Anonymous) and www.slaauk.org (Sex & Love Addicts Anonymous) and www.sauk.org (Sexaholics Anonymous).

SUGGESTIONS FOR SPIRITUAL REFLECTION

The first five readings in this section are offered for reflection. Make sure you have quiet, uninterrupted time with God and ask Him to guide you through the words and use them to speak deep into your heart. The final spiritual exercise provides an opportunity to reflect on deeper emotional needs. For those of you who enjoy Christian music, there is a recommended list of songs that can be particularly beneficial to add to your playlist when you need to R.U.N. I have also collated many of the Scriptures used throughout the book for you to reflect on and even seek to memorise.

Psalm 25 (NIV)

In you, Lord my God,
I put my trust.
I trust in you;
do not let me be put to shame,
nor let my enemies triumph over me.

No one who hopes in you
will ever be put to shame,
but shame will come on those
who are treacherous without cause.

Show me your ways, Lord,
teach me your paths.
Guide me in your truth and teach me,
for you are God my Saviour,
and my hope is in you all day long.
Remember, Lord, your great mercy and love,
for they are from of old.

Do not remember the sins of my youth
and my rebellious ways;
according to your love remember me,

for you, Lord, are good.
Good and upright is the Lord;
   therefore he instructs sinners in his ways.
He guides the humble in what is right
   and teaches them his way.

All the ways of the Lord are loving and faithful
   toward those who keep the demands of his covenant.
For the sake of your name, Lord,
   forgive my iniquity, though it is great.

Who, then, are those who fear the Lord?
   He will instruct them in the ways they should choose.
They will spend their days in prosperity,
  and their descendants will inherit the land.

The Lord confides in those who fear him;
   he makes his covenant known to them.
My eyes are ever on the Lord,
   for only he will release my feet from the snare.

Turn to me and be gracious to me,
   for I am lonely and afflicted.
Relieve the troubles of my heart
   and free me from my anguish.
Look on my affliction and my distress
   and take away all my sins.

See how numerous are my enemies
   and how fiercely they hate me!
Guard my life and rescue me;
   do not let me be put to shame,
   for I take refuge in you.

May integrity and uprightness protect me,
   because my hope, Lord, is in you.
Deliver Israel, O God,
   from all their troubles!

Be Thou My Vision, Hymn

Be Thou my Vision, O Lord of my heart;
Naught be all else to me, save that Thou art;
Thou my best Thought, by day or by night,
Waking or sleeping, Thy presence my light.

Be Thou my Wisdom, and Thou my true Word;
I ever with Thee and Thou with me, Lord;
Thou my great Father, I Thy true son;
Thou in me dwelling, and I with Thee one.

Be Thou my battle Shield, Sword for the fight;
Be Thou my Dignity, Thou my Delight;
Thou my soul's Shelter, Thou my high Tow'r:
Raise Thou me heav'nward, O Pow'r of my pow'r.

Riches I heed not, nor man's empty praise,
Thou mine Inheritance, now and always:
Thou and Thou only, first in my heart,
High King of Heaven, my Treasure Thou art.

High King of Heaven, my victory won,
May I reach Heaven's joys, O bright Heav'n's Sun!
Heart of my own heart, whate'er befall,
Still be my Vision, O Ruler of all.

The song dates from at least the eighth century, though it has often been attributed to the sixth-century Irish Christian poet Saint Dallan.

The Serenity Prayer by Reinhold Niebuhr

God grant me the serenity
To accept the things I cannot change;
Courage to change the things I can;
And wisdom to know the difference.

Living one day at a time;
Enjoying one moment at a time;
Accepting hardships as the pathway to peace;
Taking, as He did, this sinful world
As it is, not as I would have it;

Trusting that He will make all things right
If I surrender to His Will;
So that I may be reasonably happy in this life
And supremely happy with Him
Forever and ever in the next.
Amen.

Isaiah 55 - Invitation to the Thirsty (NIV)

"Come, all you who are thirsty,
come to the waters;
and you who have no money,
come, buy and eat!
Come, buy wine and milk
without money and without cost.

Why spend money on what is not bread,
and your labor on what does not satisfy?
Listen, listen to me, and eat what is good,
and you will delight in the richest of fare.

Give ear and come to me;
listen, that you may live.
I will make an everlasting covenant with you,
my faithful love promised to David.

See, I have made him a witness to the peoples,
a ruler and commander of the peoples.

Surely you will summon nations you know not,
and nations you do not know will come running to you,
because of the Lord your God,
the Holy One of Israel,
for he has endowed you with splendor."

Seek the Lord while he may be found;
call on him while he is near.

Let the wicked forsake their ways
and the unrighteous their thoughts.
Let them turn to the Lord, and he will have mercy on them,
and to our God, for he will freely pardon.
"For my thoughts are not your thoughts,
neither are your ways my ways,"
declares the Lord.

"As the heavens are higher than the earth,
so are my ways higher than your ways
and my thoughts than your thoughts.

As the rain and the snow
come down from heaven,
and do not return to it
without watering the earth
and making it bud and flourish,
so that it yields seed for the sower and bread for the eater,

so is my word that goes out from my mouth:
It will not return to me empty,
but will accomplish what I desire
and achieve the purpose for which I sent it.

You will go out in joy
and be led forth in peace;
the mountains and hills
will burst into song before you,
and all the trees of the field
will clap their hands.

Instead of the thornbush will grow the juniper,
and instead of briers the myrtle will grow.
This will be for the Lord's renown,
for an everlasting sign,
that will endure forever."

A Prayer based upon the First Principle and Foundation
(from Take & Receive Series by Bergen and Schwann)

Lord, my God, when your love spilled over into creation
You thought of me.
I am
from love, of love, for love

Let my heart, O God, always recognise,
cherish

and enjoy your goodness in all of creation.

Direct all that is me towards your praise.
Teach me reverence for every person, all things.
Energise me in your service.

Lord God,
may nothing ever distract me from your love...
neither health nor sickness,
wealth nor poverty,
honour nor dishonor
long life nor short life.

May I never seek nor choose to be other than You intend or wish.

Amen.

THE FRUITS OF THE SPIRIT EXERCISE

Read the Scripture below and take time to consider which fruits are abundant in your life.
Start by reflecting on which fruits you witnessed in childhood?
Then which you have seen and experienced in others around you?
And finally, which you struggle most to experience and share yourself?
At the end of the exercise take time to pray for the areas where you'd like to grow and ask for guidance on how to achieve this.

"The fruit of the Spirit is love, joy, peace, patience, kindness, goodness, faithfulness, gentleness and self-control." (Galatians 5:22)

THE ARMOUR OF GOD

Recovering from addiction is a battle – and every soldier knows that you don't go into battle without putting your armour on first! So read this passage from Ephesians and consider – perhaps copy it and put it on your bathroom mirror or wardrobe door so when you're getting dressed each morning, you're ready for whatever triggers you may face.

"Put on the full armour of God, so that you can take your stand against the devil's schemes. For our struggle is not against flesh and blood, but against the rulers, against the authorities, against the powers of this dark world and against the spiritual forces of evil in the heavenly realms. Therefore put on the full armour of God, so that when the day of evil comes, you may be able to stand your ground, and after you have done everything, to stand. Stand firm then, with the belt of truth buckled around your waist, with the breastplate of righteousness in place, and with your feet fitted with the readiness that comes from the gospel of peace. In addition to all this, take up the shield of faith, with which you can extinguish all the flaming arrows of the evil one.

Take the helmet of salvation and the sword of the Spirit, which is the word of God." (Ephesians 6: 10-16, NIV)

Another helpful exercise to start thinking about living out this Scripture, is to take each piece of spiritual armour and write down practical things that you can do for each of these eg. Sword of the Spirit: memorise a Bible verse a week.

CHRISTIAN MUSIC

The songs below have been kindly compiled by a group of Christian men in recovery.

Arms of Grace - Beth Croft - (Soul Suvivor/Momentum 2011)

Forever Reign - from the album *Forever Reign*, by Hillsong Worship

Boldly I Approach - by Rend Collective

At the Cross - by Chris Tomlin

I Surrender - from the album *Cornerstone*, by Hillsong Worship

Good, Good Father - by Housefires

It Is Well - from the album *You Make Me Brave*, by Bethel Music

A Little Longer - from the album *You Make Me Brave*, By Bethel Music

Wonder - from the album *You Make Me Brave*, By Bethel Music

We Dance - from the album *If We're Honest,* by Francesca Battistelli

This I Believe (The Creed) - from the album *No Other Name,* by Hillsong Worship

Calvary - from the album *No Other Name*, by Hillsong Worship

All Things Are New - from the album *No Other Name*, by Hillsong Worship

Broken Vessels (Amazing Grace) - from the album *No Other Name*, by Hillsong Worship

All Things New - from the album *No Other Name*, by Hillsong Worship

Here Now - from the album *Empires*, by Hillsong United

Here Now (Madness) - from the album *Empires*, by Hillsong United

Touch The Sky - from the album *Empires*, by Hillsong United

Street Called Mercy - from the album *Empires*, by Hillsong United

Even When It Hurts - from the album *Empires,* by Hillsong United

I'm Cradled – by David Bilbrough

Show me the Way of the Cross – by Matt Redman

Refine Me – from the album *Kansas,* by Jennifer Knapp

'40 DAY' EXERCISE

Below is a list of many of the Bible verses cited throughout the text of the book. There are 40 of them – the same number of days that Jesus was tempted in the desert. A powerful exercise would be to seek to memorise or meditate on one verse per day. Mostly I have often used translations from either the NIV (New International Version), unless I have stated otherwise can have used an alternative translation that seemed more appropriate.

As the deer pants for the water brooks, so my soul pants for thee, O God, for the living God.
(PSALM 42:1-2) NKJV

My soul thirsts for Thee, my flesh yearns for Thee, in a dry and weary land where there is not water.
(PSALM 63:1) NKJV

Blessed are those who hunger and thirst for righteousness for they will be filled.
(MATTHEW 5:6)

Jesus stood and said in a loud voice, 'If anyone is thirsty, let him come to me and drink. Whoever believes in me, as the Scripture said, streams of living water will flow from him.
(JOHN 7:37)

I am the Alpha and the Omega, the Beginning and the End. To him who is thirsty I will give to drink without cost form the spring of the water of life.
(REVELATION 21:6)

But I say to you that everyone who looks at a woman with lustful intent has already committed adultery with her in his heart.
(MATTHEW 5:28)

God created man in His own image – male and female he created them.
(GENESIS 1:27)

And the man and his wife were both naked and were not ashamed.
(GENESIS 2:25)

For I alone know the plans I have for you, plans to bring you prosperity, not disaster, plans to bring about the future you hope for.
(JEREMIAH 29:11)

Do not be afraid, for you will not be put to shame; and do not feel humiliated, for you will not be disgraced.... For your husband is your Maker, whose name is the Lord of hosts, and your redeemer is the Holy One who is called the God of all the earth.
(ISAIAH 4:5)

Trust in the Lord with all your heart and lean not on your own understanding, acknowledge him in all your ways and he will direct your paths.
(PROVERBS 3:5-6)

The Lord is close to the broken hearted, He rescues those whose spirits are crushed.
(PSALM 34:18)

I don't really understand myself, for I want to do what is right, but I don't do it. Instead I do what I hate.
(ROMANS 7:15) NLT

And we know that in all things God works for the good of those who love him.
(ROMANS 8:28)

For I am convinced that neither death nor life, neither angels nor demons, neither the present nor the future, nor any powers, neither height nor depth, nor anything else in all creation, will be able to separate us from the love of God that is in Christ Jesus our Lord.
(ROMANS 8:38-39)

If we claim to be without sin, we deceive ourselves and the truth is not in us. If we confess our sins, he is faithful and just and will forgive us our sins and purify us from all unrighteousness. If we claim we have not sinned, we make him out to be a liar and his word is not in us.
(1 JOHN 1:8-10)

Jesus said, "If you hold to my teaching, you are really my disciples. Then you will know the truth, and the truth will set you free.
(JOHN 8:31-32)

Search me, God, and know my heart; test me and know my anxious thoughts, See if there is any offensive way in me, and lead me in the way everlasting.
(PSALM 139:23-24)

Who can see his own mistakes? Forgive my sins that I do not see. And keep Your servant from sinning by going my own way. Do not let these sins rule over me. Then I will be without blame. And I will not be found guilty of big sins.
(PSALM 19:12-13)

Refrain from anger and turn from wrath; do not fret – it leads only to evil.
(PSALM 37:8) NLT
Hope deferred makes the heart sick, but desire fulfilled is the tree of life.
(PROVERBS 12:12) NASB

We must wrestle against, principalities, against powers, against the rulers of the darkness of this world, against spiritual wickedness in high places'.
(EPHESIANS 6:12) NKJV

He who conceals his transgressions will not prosper, But he who confesses and forsakes them will find compassion.
(PROVERBS 28:13)

But if we walk in the Light as He Himself is in the Light, we have fellowship with one another, and the blood of Jesus His Son cleanses us from all sin.
(1 JOHN 1:17) NKJV

Do not judge, and you will not be judged; and do not condemn, and you will not be condemned; pardon, and you will be pardoned. Give, and it will be given to you. They will pour into your lap a good measure-- pressed down, shaken together, and running over. For by your standard of measure it will be measured to you in return.
(LUKE 6:37-38)

Therefore, confess your sins to one another, and pray for one another so that you may be healed The effective prayer of a righteous man can accomplish much.
(JAMES 5:6)

Two people are better off than one, for they can help each other succeed. If one person falls, the other can reach out and help. But someone who falls alone is in real trouble. Likewise, two people lying close together can keep each other warm. But how can one be warm alone? A person standing alone can be attacked and defeated, but two can stand back-to-back and conquer. Three are even better, for a triple-braided cord is not easily broken.
(ECCLESIASTES 4:9-12) NLT

Greater is He that is in you, than he who is in the world.
(1 JOHN 4:4) NKJV

Watch and pray, lest you enter into temptation. The spirit indeed is willing, but the flesh is weak.
(MATTHEW 26:41) NKJV

Blessed is the one who perseveres under trial because, having stood the test, that person will receive the crown of life that the Lord has promised to those who love him.
(JAMES 1:12)

Dear brothers and sisters, when troubles of any kind come your way, consider it an opportunity for great joy. For you know that when your faith is tested, your endurance has a chance to grow. So let it grow, for when your endurance is fully developed, you will be perfect and complete, needing nothing.
(JAMES 1:2-4) NLT

And the God of all grace, who called you to his eternal glory in Christ, after you have suffered a little while, will himself restore you and make you strong, firm and steadfast.
(1 PETER 5:10) NLT

So be truly glad. There is wonderful joy ahead, even though you have to endure many trials for a little while. These trials will show that your faith is genuine. It is being tested as fire tests and purifies gold—though your faith is far more precious than mere gold. So when your faith remains strong through many trials, it will bring you much praise and glory and honor on the day when Jesus Christ is revealed to the whole world.
(1 PETER 1:6-7) NKJV

Submit therefore to God. Resist the devil and he will flee from you. Draw near to God and He will draw near to you.
(JAMES 4:7-8)

Love the Lord your God with all your heart and with all your soul and with all your mind and with all your strength.
(MATTHEW 12:31)

What does the LORD require of you? To act justly and to love mercy and to walk humbly with your God.
(MICAH 6:8) NKJV

Do you not know that your bodies are temples of the Holy Spirit, who is in you, whom you have received from God? You are not your own; you were bought at a price. Therefore honor God with your bodies.
(1 CORINTHIANS 6:19-20)

You keep track of all my sorrows. You have collected all my tears in your bottle. You have recorded each one in your book.
(PSALM 56:8) NLT

As far as the east is from the west, so far has he removed our transgressions from us.
(PSALM 103:12)

For I will take you out of the nations; I will gather you from all the countries and bring you back into your own land. I will sprinkle clean water on you, and you will be clean; I will cleanse you from all your impurities and from all your idols. I will give you a new heart and put a new spirit in you; I will remove from you your heart of stone and give you a heart of flesh. And I will put my Spirit in you and move you to follow my decrees and be careful to keep my laws.
(EZEKIEL 36: 24-27)

If you would like to receive further training for yourself, or for your pastoral care team or your church, contact info@nakedtruthproject.com. And if you think someone you know might benefit from our therapy resources, feel free to contact info@paulahall.co.uk to arrange a confidential discussion about appropriate options.

PAULA HALL

APPENDIX

A note for leaders

If you know someone who's struggling with sex or porn addiction, or you suspect this is a problem amongst any of your fellow Christians, then the most important thing you can do is love them. As we've seen throughout the pages of this book, addiction thrives in secrecy and shame and the Church and Church community can play a powerful role in reducing that.

Single-sex groups such as men's groups or women's breakfasts, youth meetings and small groups are all a great place to start conversations about struggles with addiction. Remember that we all struggle with dependency on things other than God and are prone to 'worship' things that give us pleasure and take away our pain. Or if you are preaching or speaking about any kind of worldy distraction from God (and there are many), being bold enough to say the word 'pornography' demonstrates the awareness that it is a real issue and one that the church wants to talk about.

Any Christian, anywhere, can offer a compassionate listening ear – never underestimate how profoundly healing it is to be able to speak honestly and openly with someone who isn't going to judge or condemn you. Remember that sex and porn addiction has very little to do with sex. You are not speaking with someone who has an out of control sex drive, but someone who is in deep emotional pain and is seeking to soothe that pain with their behaviours. Having said that, the person who's confiding in you may be confused themselves and their shame may spill over into explicit confessions because they don't yet know how to explain why they do the things they do not want to do. Remember Jesus with the woman at the well or the woman caught in adultery? He didn't ask for detail or make moral judgments about her behaviour. He knew that it stemmed from a deep hunger for what only God can supply. In John 8:7 Jesus also challenged the onlookers to 'cast the first stone' if they were without sin, because He knew that we are all sinners who can only be saved by grace.

A non-judgmental approach is equally important for partners and parents of people with sex and porn addiction. It is common for those closest to addicts to blame themselves and many fear that will be the assumption of others. Furthermore, remember that partners of people with addiction are often struggling with acute feelings of anger and betrayal, as well as fear for their future. They need a safe space to share their feelings honestly, and ongoing support for themselves, as well as help for their partners.

Depending on your experience and resources, both personally and within the church, you may be able to give further guidance and support yourself. Or you may know of a nearby church that can help. If not, do use the resources section in the previous chapter and contact The Naked Truth Project to see if there are any newer resources within your area.

Addiction is a very complicated area to help people in because it can stem from so many unaddressed, and indeed unacknowledged, psychological problems. Therefore it's essential to be ready to advise people to seek professional help if they continue to relapse. Or if giving up their addiction spirals them into depression or anxiety. Relapse is a common part of the addiction process and it's important not to assume that someone who continues to struggle either lacks motivation or faith. Remember that addiction is biological as well as psychological and spiritual and hence in the same way as you would not automatically expect a cancer patient to be healed by prayer alone, nor would you dissuade them from seeing an oncologist, the same approach with someone with chronic addiction should be taken.

PAULA HALL

APPENDIX

Naked Truth & CARE

Naked Truth

Naked Truth is the flagship initiative of Visible Ministries and seeks to open eyes and free lives from the damaging impact of pornography. Through education, awareness and recovery programmes, Naked Truth's team of communicators, educators and professional therapists work nationally with men, women and young people.

Currently, Naked Truth work in three main areas:

OUR CHILDREN:

We deliver schools programmes in secondary schools, parenting workshops, and create mentoring resources for young people.

OUR CHURCHES:

Naked Truth's online recovery groups, books, conferences, theological training, sermons and seminars provide churches with both education and practical support.

OUR COMMUNITIES:

Working alongside Parliamentarians, street artists and researchers we work to shape the national conversation regarding the social costs of pornography. At the time of print, we are currently in the development of a recovery app which will provide hope and help for any individual struggling with porn use.

Visit **www.nakedtruthproject.com** or call us on **0161 637 0240**.

CARE

CARE is a well-established, mainstream Christian charity providing resources and helping to bring Christian insight and experience to matters of public policy and practical caring initiatives. At the heart of all CARE do is the issue of Human Dignity; the belief that men and women are made in the image of God. Currently CARE is campaigning on a range of issues across the UK's Parliaments and Assemblies including; Human Trafficking, Euthanasia, Abortion, Pornography, Gambling and Family Policy.

CARE reflects the church within the nation and engages the Church of Jesus Christ in its various different expressions to be a Christian voice of truth.

Visit **www.care.org.uk** or call **0207 7233 0455**